Florida Beachfront Lodgings
The West Coast

Gail Bottone

Pineapple Press, Inc.
Sarasota, Florida

Acknowledgments

Foremost, I would like to thank my husband, Pete, for all the hours he spent helping me on this endeavor. I would also like to thank my daughters, Brittany and Kristin, for understanding my absences and enduring the research trips when they accompanied me. I am also indebted to Ron Jaudon and Donna Johnson, who offered innumerable hours of assistance.

Inquiries should be addressed to:
Pineapple Press, Inc.
P.O. Box 3899
Sarasota, Florida 34230

LIBRARY OF CONGRESS CATALOGING IN PUBLICATION DATA

Bottone, Gail, 1962–
        Florida beachfront lodgings. The West Coast / by Gail Bottone.
                p.   cm.
        ISBN 1-56164-145-6
        1. Hotels—Florida—Gulf Coast—Guidebooks. 2. Seaside resorts—Florida—Gulf Coast—Guidebooks. 3. Restaurants—Florida—Gulf Coast—Guidebooks. 4. Gulf Coast (Fla.)—Guidebooks. I. Title.
TX907.3.F62G842   1998
647.9475901—dc21   97-48385

First Edition
10 9 8 7 6 5 4 3 2 1

Design by Carol Tornatore
Printed and bound by Edwards Brothers, Ann Arbor, Michigan

Table of Contents

Suncoast Beaches

Sarasota/Manatee Beaches

Southwest Beaches

Lodgings That Accept Pets

Introduction

*L*ooking for an accommodation located directly on Florida's beautiful beaches? Well, you've come to the right source. There are literally hundreds of beachfront resorts, motels, and condominiums along Florida's west coast. I have spent the better part of two years combing the beaches along the west coast, searching for those accommodations located right on the sand. **These accommodations are not across the street from or near the beach but right on it.** (I personally visited each lodging to make sure it is a genuine beachfront location.) This guide helps take the guesswork out of planning a beach vacation. Whether you want a quaint cottage, a secluded garden apartment, or a luxurious condominium, this book will help you find the perfect spot and feel confident that you will be spending your vacation on the beach.

Vacationers on a limited budget, those with special needs, and those traveling with pets can stay on the beach, too. I found many accommodations to fit most everyone's budget. Prices per night ranged from $40 to over $125. For travelers with special needs, this guide provides limited information regarding handicapped access. To ensure that your specific needs are met, I recommend that you call ahead and inquire about available facilities. People traveling with pets will find this guide useful as I found several hotels on the beaches that do accept pets. If the accommodation does allow pets, it is noted in the amenities section of each accommodations listing. I have also included information regarding weight limits and fees, if applicable.

This guide spans Florida's entire west coast, with the exception of the Big Bend region, which is located between the Panhandle and the Suncoast beaches. This region is characterized by expansive salt marshes, hardwood hammocks, and numerous coastal rivers. While the natural rustic setting provides a backdrop for many interesting destinations, including quaint fishing villages, shops, and great seafood restaurants, there are no natural sandy beaches.

Naples Beach Hotel

I divided this book into chapters according to regions that can be traversed in a day, although the Panhandle may take two days with stops along the way. The beaches within each area are unique and worth taking the time to explore. Accommodations listed in this guide begin with the Panhandle which, unlike the rest of Florida, falls in the Central Standard Time Zone. The change from Central to Eastern Standard Time occurs near Mexico Beach (between Bay and Gulf Counties). The Panhandle region is famous for its emerald green waters and beautiful sand dunes. Because of Hurricane Opal, which hit the Panhandle in October 1995, most of the accommodations there have been newly renovated. Next is the centrally located Suncoast area, a convenient destination for those wishing to venture into either Tampa or Orlando to visit the many attractions and theme parks. Located just south of the Suncoast, across the Sunshine Skyway Bridge, are the Sarasota/Manatee beaches which offer a more laid-back atmosphere. "Gin clear" water and soft, white sand give you the feeling of being in the Caribbean. Finally, the tropical setting of the Southwest Florida beaches, accentuated with palm trees and beauti-fully flowering plants, creates the perfect atmosphere for your beach getaway.

For each geographical area, an *Overview* section describes the character of each beach/tourist area. The *Getting There* section pro-vides the names and telephone numbers of local airports, plus basic directions for arriving by car. The *Accommodations* section provides an alphabetical listing of Gulf-front lodgings and a checklist of basic information: name, address, telephone numbers, website address, total number of units, type of units, credit cards accepted, and check-in and check-out times. Various amenities are also listed: pool, hot tub, restaurant/bar, shuffleboard, fitness center, color cable televi-sion, guest laundry (coin-operated washer and dryer), grills, handi-capped access, pet allowances, conference facilities, and fax services. "TAC" means that the facility pays a Travel Agent Commission.

Specific rates are not listed. However, a pricing scale (per unit, based on double occupancy) is used. Accommodations are listed as $

(under $75), $$ ($75 to $125), and $$$ ($125+). Price ranges (indicated by $/$$, for example) are approximate and are based on peak season rates, subject to availability and subject to change without notice. Taxes are not included. Prices also vary depending on room view and space availability. Generally, Florida's seasons are as follows: peak season is January through April (highest rates); mid-season is May through August (moderate rates); and off-season is September through mid-December (lowest rates). The Panhandle is an exception; its peak season is May through August.

When planning your vacation, use the telephone numbers or websites in the listings to check specific rates. Keep in mind when choosing a type of accommodation that each facility has its own definition for each type of unit listed. Most facilities use the terms "one-bedroom apartment," "suite," "kitchenette," and "efficiency" interchangeably. Therefore, you may want to ask about specific rooms and amenities when you call.

For those travelers seeking privately owned beachfront condominiums or houses, I have provided telephone numbers of selected resort rental companies that can assist you (not available in all areas). In *Points of Interest*, I have listed activities and attractions convenient to beach areas. For serious and not-so-serious duffers, I have included a partial listing of *Semi-Private and Public Golf Courses* located within each beach region. The *Dining Out* section gives you a quick reference list of restaurants to sample. Most listed are either my favorites or those recommended by friends and "locals."

This guide contains other useful information intended to help make your beach vacation even more enjoyable. For the fisherman, information regarding fishing regulations and an identification page of fish commonly found in the Gulf of Mexico is provided. Vacationers interested in shelling will find the shell identification page useful. A listing of the area chambers of commerce is provided for anyone needing additional information.

It is important to note that while this guide provides a comprehensive list of beachfront accommodations, it is certainly not all-inclusive. The sheer number of beachfront units makes it virtually impossible to list every accommodation. Remember, there are over 600 miles of coastline along Florida's west coast! If you find an accommodation that I have overlooked and would like to see it in the next edition, please send me the name and telephone number of the lodging and I will be happy to research it. Send your suggestions to:

Gail Bottone
P.O. Box 273971
Tampa, FL 33688-3971

Have a great vacation in Florida, under the sun and on the beach!

Fishing Regulations

Florida requires everyone who fishes to have a license, with the following exceptions: persons under age sixteen, persons fishing from a licensed boat, and Florida residents fishing from a pier. Fishing licenses can be purchased at sporting goods stores and in the sporting goods department of many discount stores.

For more information regarding fishing regulations contact the following agencies:

Fresh Water

Game and Fresh Water Fish Commission
620 South Meridian Street
Tallahassee, FL 32399-1600
(904) 488-1960

Salt Water

Department of Natural Resources
Marjory Stoneman Douglas Building
3900 Commonwealth Boulevard
Tallahassee, FL 32399-1600
(904) 488-6327

Black Drum	Speckled Trout	Spanish Mackeral	Flounder
Cobia	Snook	Snapper	Ladyfish
Pompano	Pinfish	Sheepshead	Tarpon

Shelling Regulations

The collection of empty shells that have washed up on the beach is a favorite pastime of many Florida visitors, and the west coast beaches offer a wide variety of beautiful specimens. However, many beaches in Florida have regulations regarding the collection of shells containing live animals. For example, the city of Sanibel strictly prohibits live shelling because of a depletion of the area's natural resources. Contact the Parks and Recreation Department in the area you're staying to check local regulations.

Brown Cockle

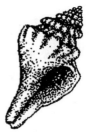

Counch

Duck Clam

Periwinkle

Rose Cockle

Turkey Wing

Driving Distances Between Selected Cities

DRIVING DISTANCES — Mileage between selected cities	BRADENTON	CLEARWATER	COCOA BEACH	DAYTONA BEACH	FORT LAUDERDALE	FORT MYERS	JACKSONVILLE	KEY WEST	KISSIMMEE	MIAMI	NAPLES	OCALA	ORLANDO	PANAMA CITY	PENSACOLA	SARASOTA	ST. PETERSBURG	TALLAHASSEE
W. PALM BEACH	176	215	122	187	43	124	274	219	150	64	147	233	166	493	587	174	200	401
TAMPA	41	22	122	139	234	123	188	387	74	245	156	93	85	331	425	53	20	239
TALLAHASSEE	272	235	288	234	444	356	163	606	255	463	389	170	242	97	191	285	250	—
ST. PETERSBURG	26	19	142	159	234	110	208	379	95	245	143	113	105	342	435	39	—	250
SARASOTA	13	55	164	181	201	71	236	341	116	211	105	142	127	377	471	—	39	285
PENSACOLA	458	421	473	425	630	541	354	792	441	649	575	356	428	103	—	471	435	191
PANAMA CITY	364	327	380	331	536	448	260	698	347	555	481	262	334	—	103	377	342	97
ORLANDO	114	106	46	54	209	153	134	371	18	228	187	72	—	334	428	127	105	242
OCALA	129	103	118	76	276	195	95	436	87	294	229	—	72	262	356	142	113	170
NAPLES	117	159	222	241	105	34	319	236	175	107	—	229	187	481	575	105	143	389
MIAMI	220	260	186	251	22	141	338	155	212	—	107	294	228	555	649	211	245	463
KISSIMMEE	103	96	51	71	193	141	152	355	—	212	175	87	18	347	441	116	95	255
KEY WEST	353	395	340	405	177	270	493	—	355	155	236	436	371	698	792	341	379	606
JACKSONVILLE	223	197	153	89	317	285	—	493	152	338	319	95	134	260	354	236	208	163
FORT MYERS	84	125	190	207	133	—	285	270	141	141	34	195	153	448	541	71	110	356
FT. LAUDERDALE	209	249	165	229	—	133	317	177	193	22	105	276	209	536	630	201	234	444
DAYTONA BEACH	168	160	65	—	229	207	89	405	71	251	241	76	54	331	425	181	159	234
COCOA BEACH	151	143	—	65	165	190	153	340	51	186	222	118	46	380	473	164	142	288
CLEARWATER	42	—	143	160	249	125	197	395	96	260	159	103	106	327	421	55	19	235
BRADENTON	—	42	151	168	209	84	223	353	103	220	117	129	114	364	458	13	26	272

Panhandle Beaches

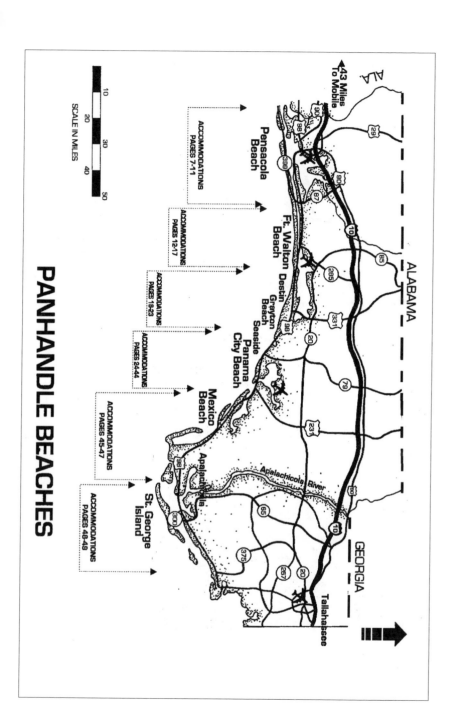

PANHANDLE BEACHES

Overview

$\mathcal{T}$he northwest region of Florida, commonly known as the Panhandle, is famous for its white, sandy beaches and clear, sparkling, emerald green waters. As you travel along US Highway 98 from Pensacola Beach to Panama City Beach, you will marvel at the beautiful rolling sand dunes topped with clusters of sea oats. The snow-white sand is a product of geological processes that resulted in Appalachian Mountain quartz crystals being deposited along the Gulf of Mexico via rivers. These crystals were broken down, washed, bleached, ground, and polished into millions of grains of sand.

Pensacola is on the western border of Florida, at the tip of the Panhandle. Pensacola Beach is a barrier island with a variety of social atmospheres ranging from casual to elegant. Much of Pensacola Beach is protected from development, giving the area a strong, natural ambiance. There is plenty to do there. Watersports abound near the beaches, and you can rent just about any mode of transportation including bicycles, mopeds, and rollerblades. Visitors can also choose from a multitude of dining and shopping experiences.

Continuing east on Highway 98 from Pensacola Beach, you will encounter the seaside towns of Fort Walton Beach (Okaloosa Island) and Destin, famous for their twenty-four miles of gorgeous waters and sand so soft it squeaks beneath your feet. This area is also known as the "World's Luckiest Fishing Village," boasting five saltwater fishing world records. Many deep-sea fishing charters originate from the marina at Fort Walton Beach. Opportunities for parasailing, water skiing, and windsurfing offer the adventuresome an action-packed time.

You will find more beautiful sand and water on the pristine beaches of South Walton. Eighteen distinct beach communities—including Santa Rosa Beach, Grayton Beach, Seagrove Beach, and Seaside—comprise this twenty-six mile stretch. Grayton carries the distinction of being rated the nation's finest beach. Seaside, with its brick streets and picket fences, has received international recognition for its architecture exemplifying the small-town charm of yesteryear. You won't find any fast-food restaurants or T-shirt shops in Seaside. However, you will find unique shops and great restaurants, ranging from casual to gourmet dining.

The pace picks up as you head into the Panama City Beach area. Families will find entertainment and activities to suit everyone's interests. The area offers jetskiing, parasailing, snorkeling, scuba diving, fishing, and more. You can even rent a dune buggy. The stretch of beach known as the "Miracle Strip" houses an amusement park and water theme park that provide fun and entertainment both day and night. If you seek a quieter atmosphere, the west end of Panama City Beach is definitely the place to go.

For even more peace and quiet, head east to the sleepy towns of Mexico Beach and St. George Island. (Remember as you cross the Bay County line into Gulf County to set your clocks ahead one hour as you will then be on Eastern Standard Time.) Mexico Beach, thirty miles east of Panama City on US 98, offers beautiful beaches with a few shops and restaurants. Experience Florida as it once was as you saunter down secluded beaches, hunt for shells along the shore, or fish from the surf or the city pier.

St. George Island is accessible by the GIA toll bridge and is a great destination for those who consider relaxation the main emphasis of their vacation. This area has only one motel on the beach; all other accommodations are rental houses. Although the island has only a few restaurants, more can be found in nearby Appalachicola, world-famous for oysters and seafood.

Climate

(Temperature by Degrees Farenheight)

SEASON	AVERAGE LOW	AVERAGE HIGH	GULF WATER
January–March	44	73	50s–60s
April–June	58	85	70s
July–September	71	89	80s
October–December	48	83	60s–70s

Getting There

By Air

Okaloosa County Air Terminal
(850) 651-7160
Location: One mile east of Destin

Panama City–Bay County International Airport
(850) 763-6751
Location: Four miles northwest of Panama City

Pensacola Regional Airport
(850) 435-1746
Location: Three miles northeast of Pensacola

Tallahassee Regional Airport
(904) 891-7800
Location: Five miles southwest of Tallahassee

By Car

INTERSTATE 75 or INTERSTATE 95: From I-75 or I-95 traveling north or south, take Interstate 10 West. Exit onto 319 South outside of Tallahassee to US 98 to get to St. George Island and Mexico Beach.

Proceeding on I-10 west of Tallahassee, exit onto 231 South to reach Panama City Beach or exit onto 331 South to reach Seaside and Grayton Beach. Further west on I-10, exit onto 285 South to access the Fort Walton Beach/Destin area. I-10 passes directly through Pensacola.

Pensacola Beach

Accommodations

↩ Clarion Suites Resort & Convention Center

20 Via De Luna Drive
Pensacola Beach, FL 32561
(850) 932-4300
(850) 934-9112 (fax)
(800) 874-5303
http://www.jmerealty.com

The Clarion has eighty-six unique Gulf-side suites. All suites have a separate bedroom, living room with sleeper sofa, kitchenette, and two televisions.

- TAC $/$$$
- 86 Units
- Suites
- Pool
- Color Cable TV
- Guest Laundry
- Handicapped Access
- Fitness Center
- Conference Facilities
- Fax Services
- Mastercard, VISA, Discover, American Express
- Check-in: 3 P.M. Check-out: 11 A.M.

Clarion Suites Resort

✆ Five Flags Inn

299 Fort Pickens Road
Pensacola Beach, FL 32561
(850) 932-3586
(850) 934-0257 (fax)

The Five Flags Inn has rooms with one king-size bed or two double beds. All guest rooms have entrances from the beach side and a beautiful view of the Gulf.

- TAC $$
- 49 Units
- Motel rooms
- Pool
- Color Cable TV
- Grills
- Fax Services
- Mastercard, VISA, Discover, American Express
- Check-in: 3 P.M. Check-out: 11 A.M.

✆ Hampton Inn Pensacola Beach

2 Via De Luna
Pensacola Beach, FL 32561
(850) 932-6800
(850) 932-6833 (fax)
(800) 320-8108

The Hampton Inn is Pensacola Beach's newest and largest beachfront resort. The rooms have an outstanding Gulf view, microwave, refrigerator, and voicemail messaging. Complimentary breakfast buffet is available daily. Meeting facilities can accommodate up to 300 people.

- TAC $$/$$$
- 181 Units
- Motel rooms
- Pool
- Color Cable TV
- Guest Laundry
- Handicapped Access
- Restaurant/Bar
- Fitness Center
- Conference Facilities
- Fax Services
- Mastercard, VISA, Discover, American Express
- Check-in: 4 P.M. Check-out: 11 A.M.

☞ Sans Souci

999 Ft. Pickens Road, Suite 105
Pensacola Beach, FL 32561
(850) 934-8347
(850) 934-6569 (fax)
(800) 567-0765

Sans Souci has one-, two- and three-bedroom units fully equipped with everything you need except food and drink. Most rooms have a direct view of the Gulf. A tennis court is available for guest use.

- $$
- 64 Units
- One-, two- and three-bedroom apartments with fully equipped kitchens
- Pool
- Color Cable TV

- Guest Laundry
- Grills
- Handicapped Access
- Fax Services
- No Credit Cards
- Check-in: 3 P.M. Check-out: 10 A.M.

Resort Rental Companies

Gulf Coast Accommodations
Pensacola Beach
(800) 239-4334

Tristan Realty Inc.
Pensacola Beach
(800) 445-9931

Points of Interest

Big Lagoon State Recreation Area
12301 Gulf Beach Highway
Pensacola, FL 32507
(850) 492-1595
Boating (boat ramp), campsites, canoeing, hiking trails, swimming, fishing

Perdido Key State Recreation Area
12301 Gulf Beach Highway
Pensacola, FL 32428
(850) 492-1595
Hiking trails, swimming

National Museum of Naval Aviation
1750 Radford Drive
Naval Air Station
Pensacola, FL 32508
(850) 453-2389
(800) 327-5002
The museum has everything from biplanes and blimps to fighter craft and the Skylab Command Module.
Hours: 9 A.M. to 5 P.M., daily (except Thanksgiving, Christmas and New Year's Eve)
Admission: Free

Dining Out

Flora-Bama Lounge and Package
(located on the Florida / Alabama border)
17401 Perdido Key Drive
Perdido Key
(850) 492-0611
Hours: 9 A.M. to 2:30 A.M
Gulf-front oyster bar, oysters (steamed, Cajun), shrimp, all-beef hot dogs, specials; live entertainment
Lunch: $2.80 to $8.88
Dinner: $2.80 to $8.88

Marchelo's Italian Restaurant
(located at the foot of the NAS bridge)
620 South Navy Boulevard
Pensacola
(850) 456-5200

Hours: 11 A.M. to 10 P.M.; Monday, 5 P.M. to 10 P.M.; closed Tuesday
Features: pasta, seafood, steak; casual dress
Lunch: $3.96 to $6.75
Dinner: $7.50 to $15.95

Sandshaker Lounge & Package and Sandshaker Sandwich Shop
731 Pensacola Beach Boulevard
Pensacola Beach
(850) 932-0023 Sandwich Shop
(850) 932-2211 Lounge
Hours: 11 A.M. to 5 P.M., Monday through Wednesday; 11 A.M. to 9 P.M.,
Thursday to Sunday (sandwich shop)
Features: sandwiches, salads, daily specials; casual dining
Lunch: $4.50 to $5
Dinner: $4.50 to $5

Seville Quarter
130 East Government Street
Pensacola
(850) 434-6211
Hours: 11 A.M. to 2:30 P.M., 5 P.M. to 11 P.M.; Sunday brunch, 11 A.M. to
2:30 P.M.; bars open until 2:30 A.M.
Features: entertainment complex in one New Orleans–style building,
one restaurant, and seven bars; live entertainment

Okaloosa Island/Fort Walton Beach

Accommodations

☞ The Breakers of Fort Walton Beach

381 Santa Rosa Boulevard
Fort Walton Beach, FL 32548
(850) 244-9127
(850) 244-4277 (fax)
(800) 395-4853

The Breakers is a high-rise condominium complex with luxurious one-, two- and three- bedroom floor plans, all with breathtaking views of the Gulf. Each unit is completely equipped with two televisions, VCR, dishwasher, microwave, refrigerator with ice maker, washer and dryer, and private balcony. There is a tennis court on the property.

- $$$
- 189 Units
- One-, two- and three-bedroom condominiums
- Pool
- Color Cable TV
- Guest Laundry
- Sandwich Shop
- Shuffleboard
- Fitness Center
- Conference Facilities
- Fax Services
- Mastercard, VISA, Discover, American Express
- Check-in: 3 P.M. Check-out: 10 A.M.

☞ Days Inn & Suites

573 Santa Rosa Boulevard
Fort Walton Beach, FL 32548
(850) 244-8686
(850) 244-5926 (fax)
(800) 238-8686

The Days Inn & Suites offers seven-story high rise towers, as well as poolside apartments and beachfront townhouses. This unique apartment/hotel provides the convenience of condominium living with the services of a first class hotel. All rooms have ceramic tile and carpet.

- TAC $$/$$$
- 180 Units
- Suites; one- and two-bedroom apartments with fully equipped kitchens
- Pool
- Color Cable TV

- Guest Laundry
- Fax Services
- Mastercard, VISA, Discover, American Express
- Check-in 3 P.M. Check-out: 11 A.M.

☜ Nautilus Condominiums

660 Nautilus Court
Fort Walton Beach, FL 32548
(850) 244-6900
(850) 244-6975 (fax)
(800) 328-8039

The Nautilus Condominiums are a modern, seven-story condominium complex. All units have balconies overlooking the Gulf and their own washer and dryer.

- $$$
- 8 Units
- One-, two- and three-bedroom condominiums
- Pool
- Color Cable TV

- Grills
- Fax Services
- Mastercard, VISA, Discover, American Express
- Check-in: 3 P.M. Check-out: 10 A.M.

☜ Radisson Beach Resort

1110 Santa Rosa Boulevard
Fort Walton Beach, FL 32548
(850) 243-9181
(850) 664-7652 (fax)
(800) 732-4853

The Radisson has 402 luxurious guest rooms, three pools, poolside tiki bar, two lighted tennis courts, beach volleyball, and 10,000 square feet of meeting/banquet space. The hotel is within walking distance of restaurants, outlet shopping, and area attractions.

- TAC $/$$$
- 402 Units
- Motel rooms and suites
- Pool
- Color Cable TV
- Guest Laundry
- Handicapped Access

- Restaurant/Bar
- Fitness Center
- Conference Facilities
- Fax Services
- Mastercard, VISA, Discover, American Express
- Check-in: 4 P.M. Check-out: 11 A.M.

✆ **Ramada Plaza Beach Resort**
1500 Miracle Strip Parkway
Fort Walton Beach, FL 32548
(850) 243-9161
(850) 244-5763 (fax)
(800) 874-8962

The Ramada Plaza Beach Resort boasts four pools, three restaurants, and two lounges. All rooms feature one king-size bed or two double beds.

- TAC $$
- 335 Units
- Motel rooms and suites
- Pool
- Hot Tub
- Color Cable TV
- Guest Laundry
- Grills

- Handicapped Access
- Restaurant/Bar
- Pets (under 25 pounds; $15 per stay)
- Fitness Center
- Conference Facilities
- Fax Services
- Mastercard, VISA, Discover, American Express
- Check-in: 3 P.M. Check-out: 11 A.M.

✆ **Rodeway Inn**
866 Santa Rosa Boulevard
Fort Walton Beach, FL 32548
(850) 243-3114
(850) 664-5431 (fax)
(800) 458-8552

The accommodations at the Rodeway Inn are spacious and tastefully decorated. Two of the units have Jacuzzi tubs.

- TAC $$
- 140 Units
- Motel rooms and efficiencies with fully equipped kitchens
- Pool
- Color Cable TV

- Fax Services
- Mastercard, VISA, Discover, American Express
- Check-in: 2 P.M. Check-out: 10 A.M.

❧ Sheraton Four Points Hotel
1325 Miracle Strip Parkway
Fort Walton Beach, FL 32548
(850) 243-8116
(850) 244-3064 (fax)
(800) 874-8104

The Sheraton Four Points Hotel will complete a brand new seven-story building in May of 1998. Guests are offered sparkling rooms with coffee makers, refrigerators, microwaves, and ironing boards. Most rooms overlook the lushly landscaped courtyard and pool area consisting of two pools and two hot tubs.

- TAC $$
- 217 Units
- Motel rooms and suites
- Pool
- Hot Tub
- Color Cable TV
- Guest Laundry
- Handicapped Access

- Restaurant
- Fitness Center
- Conference Facilities
- Fax Services
- Mastercard, VISA. Discover, American Express
- Check-in: 3 P.M. Check-out: 12 P.M.

Resort Rental Companies

Abbott Resorts
Destin (rentals available in Fort Walton Beach)
(800) 336-GULF
e-mail: rentals@abbott-resorts.com

Points of Interest

Gulf Islands National Seashore
1801 Gulf Breeze Parkway

Sheraton Four Points Hotel

Gulf Breeze, FL 32561
(850) 934-2600
Campsites, fishing, hiking trails, swimming
OKALOOSA AREA: US Highway 98, a few miles east of Fort Walton Beach
Hours: 8 A.M. to sunset, daily
SANTA ROSA AREA: State Highway 399 on Santa Rosa Island
Hours: 8 A.M. to sunset, daily
Admission: Fee for day-use area

FORT PICKENS AREA: State Highway 399 to Fort Pickens Road
Hours: 7 A.M. to 10 P.M., daily
Admission: Fee for day-use area and campground; camping reservations (800) 365-2267

Gulfarium
1010 Miracle Strip Parkway
Fort Walton Beach, FL 32548
(850) 244-5169

Features performances of trained dolphins and sea lions; undersea life can be viewed through windows

Hours: Spring/summer, 9 A.M. to 6 P.M.; fall/winter, 9 A.M. to 4 P.M.

Admission: Adults, $12; seniors, $10; children ages 4 to 11, $8; children 3 and under, free

---

Dining Out

Fudpucker's Beachside Bar and Grill
108 Santa Rosa Boulevard
Fort Walton Beach
(850) 243-3833
http://www.emeraldcoast.com/~fudpuckers
Hours: 11 A.M. to 11 P.M.
Features: seafood, sandwiches, salads; casual island atmosphere
Lunch: $5 to $8
Dinner: $13 to $20

Old Bay Steamer
1310 Miracle Strip Parkway
Fort Walton Beach
(850) 664-2795
Hours: 4 P.M. to 10 P.M.
Features: seafood, steak, sandwiches; casual relaxed atmosphere
Dinner: $9.95 to $65 (for three)

Sam's Oyster House
1214 Siebert Street (north of 98 on Okaloosa Island)
Fort Walton Beach
(850) 244-3474
Hours: 11 A.M. to 10 P.M.; Friday and Saturday, 11 A.M. to 11 P.M.
Features: famous for oysters and fresh seafood; seafood buffet on weekends, steak, daily specials, children's menu; live entertainment; casual dining
Lunch: $4.75 to $5
Dinner: $7.99 to $15

Destin

Accommodations

✍ Frangista Beach Inn
1860 Old Highway 98
Destin, FL 32541
(850) 654-5501
(850) 654-5876 (fax)
(800) 382-2612

The Frangista Beach Inn has the charming character of an old, established beach hotel combined with new contemporary conventions and furnishings. Clay tile floors, tongue-and-groove paneling, color-washed furnishings, and Andirondack chairs welcome you. The newspaper is delivered daily to your door, and a continental breakfast is served each morning. Telephones have data ports for laptop PCs and faxes. Most rooms have balconies overlooking the Gulf.

- $$/$$$
- 53 Units
- Motel rooms; one- and two-bedroom suites with fully equipped kitchens; two- and four-bedroom cottages
- Pool
- Hot Tub

- Color Cable TV
- Handicapped Access
- Restaurant/Bar
- Pets
- Fax Services
- Mastercard, VISA, Discover, American Express
- Check-in: 3 P.M. Check-out: 11 A.M.

✍ Holiday Inn
1020 Highway 98 East
Destin, FL 32541
(850) 837-6181
(850) 837-1523 (fax)
(800) HOLIDAY

The Holiday Inn Destin is a newly renovated property with two buildings—a four-floor Holidome and a nine-floor tower—offering two pools, game room, two lounges, gift shop, tennis courts, and a children's activity program.

- TAC $$$
- 233 Units
- Motel rooms
- Pool
- Jacuzzi
- Color Cable TV
- Handicapped Access
- Restaurant/Bar
- Fitness Center
- Conference Facilities
- Fax Services
- Mastercard, VISA, Discover, American Express
- Check-in: 3 P.M. Check-out: 11 A.M.

⚬ Sandestin

9300 Highway 98 West
Destin, FL 32541
(850) 267-8150
(850) 267-8222 (fax)
(800) 277-0800
http://www.sandestin.com

The Sandestin is a huge, full-service resort offering tastefully appointed one-, two-, three-, and four-bedroom units in settings ranging from high-rise towers overlooking the Gulf, to the Bayside Inn at Sandestin, to secluded villas nestled along golf fairways.

- TAC $$$
- 600 Units
- Motel rooms and condominiums
- Pool
- Hot Tub
- Color Cable TV
- Guest Laundry
- Grills
- Handicapped Access
- Restaurant/Bar
- Fitness Center
- Conference Facilities
- Fax Services
- Mastercard, VISA, Discover, American Express
- Check-in: 4 P.M. Check-out: 11 A.M.

Sandestin

Sea Oats Motel & Management Company

3420 Scenic Highway 98 East
Destin, FL 32540
(850) 837-6655
(850) 654-8255 (fax)
(888) SEA-OATS
http://www.emeraldcoast.com

The Sea Oats Motel offers pretty, two-story buildings with clean, spacious accommodations. Each unit has a balcony or deck overlooking the Gulf.

- $$/$$$
- 80 Units
- Motel rooms and efficiencies with fully equipped kitchens
- Pool
- Color Cable TV
- Grills
- Fax Services
- Mastercard, VISA, Discover
- Check-in: 3 P.M. Check-out: 10 A.M.

Silver Beach Hotel

1050 Highway 98
Destin, FL 32541
(850) 837-6125
(850) 650-0962 (fax)

The Silver Beach Hotel offers family-oriented, one- and two-bedroom cottages that sleep four to six people. The one-bedroom cottage has one king-size bed, a living room with two sleeper sofas, and a kitchen. The two-bedroom cottage offers an additional bedroom with two twin beds.

- TAC $$/$$$
- 72 Units
- Motel rooms and cottages
- Pool
- Color Cable TV
- Grills
- Fax Services
- Mastercard, VISA
- Check-in: 3 P.M. Check-out: 11 A.M.

Resort Rental Companies

Abbott Resorts
Destin
(800) 336-4853
e-mail: rentals@abbott-resorts.com

dale e peterson
Destin
(800) 336-9669
e-mail: deprealty@destinfl.com

Sea Oats Management Company
Destin
(888) SEA-OATS

Henderson Beach State Recreation Area
17000 Emerald Coast Parkway
Destin, FL 32541
(850) 837-7550
Fishing, swimming

Grayton Beach State Recreation Area
Route 2
Santa Rosa Beach, FL 32459
(850) 231-4210
Boating (boat ramp), campsites, fishing, hiking trails, swimming

Seaside
County Road 30 A
PO Box 4730
Seaside, FL 32459
(850) 231-2222
Seaside is a quaint town featuring red brick streets lined with picket fences. Shops and restaurants are located at the town center.

Dining Out

AJ's Seafood and Oyster Bar
116 Northeast Highway 98
Quarter mile east of Destin Bridge
Destin
(850) 837-1913
Hours: 11 A.M. until ?
Features: seafood, children's menu; live entertainment; casual dockside dining, family atmosphere
Lunch: $5.95 to $7.95
Dinner: $9 to $35

Joe's Crab Shack
14055 Emerald Coast Parkway

Destin
(850) 650-1882
Hours: 11 A.M. to 11 P.M.
Features: seafood, steak, chicken, daily lunch specials (Monday through Friday); children's play area (Rug Rat Zone); casual dining
Lunch: $4.99 to $6.99
Dinner: $4.99 to $14.99

Landry's Seafood House
14059 Emerald Coast Parkway
Destin
(850) 650-1881
Hours: 4 P.M. to 10:15 P.M., Monday; 11 A.M. to 10:15 P.M., Tuesday through Thursday; 11 A.M. to 11:15 P.M., Friday and Saturday; 11 A.M. to 10:15 P.M., Sunday
Features: seafood, steak, chicken, pasta, children's menu; casual dining in a traditional 1940s seafood house atmosphere
Lunch: $4.99 to $8.99
Dinner: $5.99 to $25.99

Marina Cafe (overlooking Destin Harbor)
404 East Highway 98
Destin
(850) 837-7960
Hours: 5 P.M. to 10:30 P.M., bar open until 11:30 P.M.
Features: seafood, duck, chicken, steak; chef creates new menu daily; adult contemporary casual dining
Dinner: $16 to $24

Panama City Beach

Accommodations

☞ Allen's Gulfside Apartments

9622 Beach Boulevard
Panama City Beach, FL 32408
(850) 234-3527

Allen's Gulfside Apartments is a charming, newly renovated, three-story house. All rooms have a beautiful view of the Gulf and private porches or patios. Some units have a washer and dryer, dishwasher, and garbage disposal.

- $$/$$$
- 6 units
- One- and two-bedroom apartments with fully equipped kitchens
- Color Cable TV
- Guest Laundry
- Grills
- No Credit Cards
- Check-in: 2 P.M. Check-out: 10 A.M.

☞ Best Western Casa Loma

11127 Front Beach Road
Panama City Beach, FL 32407
(850) 230-3400 ext. 414
(850) 235-0888 (fax)
(800) 633-0266 (Paradise Bound Resorts)

The Best Western Casa Loma offers all Gulf-front rooms with private balconies. Coffee is available in the lobby twenty-four hours a day. The hotel is centrally located to area attractions, dining, and entertainment.

- TAC $$/$$$
- 100 Units
- Motel rooms, suites, and efficiencies with fully equipped kitchens
- Pool

- Color Cable TV
- Fax Services
- Mastercard, VISA, Discover, American Express
- Check-in: 4 P.M. Check-out: 11 A.M.

∞ Best Western Del Coronado

11127 Front Beach Road
Panama City Beach, FL 32407
(850) 230-3400
(850) 235-0888 (fax)
(800) 633-0266 (Paradise Bound Resorts)

The Best Western Del Coronado, located in the heart of the Miracle Strip, is newly renovated in a tropical decor and offers some Gulf-front rooms.

- TAC $$/$$$
- 100 Units
- Motel rooms, suites, and efficiencies with fully equipped kitchens
- Pool
- Color Cable TV
- Handicapped Access
- Conference Facilities
- Fax Services
- Mastercard, VISA, Discover, American Express
- Check-in: 4 P.M. Check-out: 11 A.M.

Best Western Del Coronado

⬪ Bikini Beach Resort

11001 Front Beach Road
Panama City Beach, FL 32407
(850) 234-3392
(850) 233-2921 (fax)
(800) 451-5307

The Bikini Beach Resort has Gulf-front rooms with spectacular views, a full game room, and a beautiful pool and poolside bar right on the Gulf.

- TAC $$
- 85 Units
- Motel rooms and efficiencies with fully equipped kitchens
- Pool
- Color Cable TV
- Guest Laundry
- Grills
- Restaurant/Bar
- Shuffleboard
- Conference Facilities
- Fax Services
- Mastercard, VISA, Discover, American Express
- Check-in: 2 P.M. Check-out: 11 A.M.

⬪ Casa Blanca Resort

11115 Front Beach Road
Panama City Beach, FL 32407
(850) 234-5245
(800) 488-6230

Most of the units at the family-oriented Casa Blanca Resort feature a separate bedroom with a queen-size bed, and a queen-size sleeper sofa in the living area.

- $$
- 35 Units
- One- and two-bedroom apartments with fully equipped kitchens
- Pool
- Hot Tub
- Color Cable TV
- Guest Laundry
- Grills
- Mastercard, VISA, Discover, American Express
- Check-in: 3 P.M. Check-out: 10 A.M.

☞ Chateau Motel

12525 Front Beach Road
Panama City Beach, FL 32407
(850) 234-2174
(850) 234-5993 (fax)
(800) 874-8826
http://www.chateau-motel.com

The Chateau has 152 newly renovated Gulf-view rooms. Centrally located, the Chateau is within walking distance of area amusements, shopping, and dining establishments.

- $$
- 152 Units
- Motel rooms and suites
- Pool
- Color Cable TV
- Guest Laundry
- Grills
- Shuffleboard
- Fax Services
- Mastercard, VISA, Discover, American Express
- Check-in: 3 P.M. Check-out: 10 A.M.

☞ Days Inn Beach

12818 Front Beach Road
Panama City Beach, FL 32407
(850) 230-3400 ext. 414
(850) 235-0888 (fax)
(800) 633-0266 (Paradise Bound Resorts)

The Days Inn offers all Gulf-front rooms with private balconies. The hotel boasts a seven-story lagoon-style waterfall pool and Jacuzzi, and a poolside bar and grill.

- TAC $$/$$$
- 188 Units
- Motel rooms, suites, and efficiencies with fully equipped kitchens
- Pool
- Hot Tub
- Color Cable TV
- Guest Laundry
- Handicapped Access
- Bar
- Conference Facilities
- Fax Services
- Mastercard, VISA, Discover, American Express
- Check-in: 4 P.M. Check-out: 11 A.M.

Days Inn Beach

☙ Desert Palms Motel
17729 Front Beach Road
Panama City Beach, FL 32413
(850) 234-2140
(850) 235-7965 (fax)
(800) 279-0080

In addition to motel-type units, the family-oriented Desert Palms
Motel also offers two Gulf-front townhouses located next to the
motel.

- TAC $/$$
- 39 Units
- Motel rooms and efficiencies
  with fully equipped kitchens
- Pool
- Color Cable TV

- Guest Laundry
- Grills
- Mastercard, VISA, Discover,
  American Express
- Check-in: 2 P.M. Check-out: 10 A.M.

∅ Edgewater Beach Resort

11212 Front Beach Road
Panama City Beach, FL 32444
(850) 235-4044
(850) 233-7529 (fax)
(800) 874-8686

The Edgewater Beach Resort is an all-inclusive, 110-acre property featuring beautiful and spacious one-, two- and three-bedroom condominiums. The pool area is nicely landscaped.

- TAC $$$
- 520 Units
- Condominiums
- Pool
- Hot Tub
- Color Cable TV
- Guest Laundry
- Grills
- Handicapped Access
- Fax Services
- Mastercard, VISA, Discover, American Express
- Check-in: 4 P.M. Check-out: 10 A.M.

∅ Emerald Beach Motel

14701 Front Beach Road
Panama City Beach, FL 32413
(850) 234-2147
(850) 235-0917 (fax)
(800) 633-3131
http://www.panamafamilyvacation.com

Emerald Beach has newly renovated one- and two-bedroom efficiencies. The building is beautiful and the grounds are well maintained.

- $$
- 78 Units
- Motel rooms and efficiencies with fully equipped kitchens
- Pool
- Color Cable TV
- Grills
- Shuffleboard
- Fax Services
- Mastercard, VISA, Discover, American Express
- Check-in: 2 P.M. Check-out: 10 A.M.

✆ Flamingo Motel

15525 Front Beach Road
Panama City Beach, FL 32413
(850) 234-2232
(850) 234-8191 (fax)
(800) 828-0400

No matter what your budget, the newly renovated Flamingo Motel has the perfect room for you. Rooms are tastefully decorated and accommodate two to eight people.

- $/$$
- 69 Units
- Motel rooms; one- and two-bedroom apartments with fully equipped kitchens
- Pool
- Color Cable TV
- Guest Laundry
- Grills
- Fax Services
- Mastercard, VISA, Discover, American Express
- Check-in: 1 P.M. Check-out: 10 A.M.

✆ Fontaine Bleau Terrace

14401 Front Beach Road
Panama City Beach, FL 32413
(850) 234-6581
(850) 235-0340 (fax)
(800) 874-8025
http://www.members.aol.com/panbchfree/beach/fbleau.htm

The Fountain Bleau has efficiencies with Gulf views. Rooms can accommodate up to four people.

- $$
- 124 Units
- Efficiencies with fully equipped kitchens
- Pool (indoor)
- Color TV
- Guest Laundry
- Fax Services
- Mastercard, VISA, Discover, American Express
- Check-in: 3 P.M. Check-out: 11 A.M.

∞ Georgian Terrace

14415 Front Beach Road
Panama City Beach, FL 32413
(850) 234-2144
(850) 234-8413 (fax)

The Georgian Terrace is family owned and operated. All rooms are spacious and have private enclosed porches. The motel features an enclosed heated pool.

- $/$$
- 28 Units
- One- and two-bedroom apartments with fully equipped kitchens
- Pool
- Color Cable TV
- Grills
- Handicapped Access
- Shuffleboard
- Fax Services
- Mastercard, VISA, Discover, American Express
- Check-in: 2 P.M. Check-out: 11 A.M.

∞ Gulf Edge Inn

9704 Beach Boulevard
Panama City Beach, FL 32408
(850) 234-5683

The Gulf Edge Inn is a small, quiet, "old-time" Florida beachfront getaway offering clean, simple and inexpensive accommodations.

- $
- 8 Units
- One- and two-bedroom apartments with fully equipped kitchens
- Color Cable TV
- Grills
- Pets ($100 deposit; $10 per day, $25 per week)
- Mastercard, VISA Check-in: 3 P.M.
- Check-out: 11 A.M.

∞ Gulf View Motel

14501 Front Beach Road
Panama City Beach, FL 32413
(850) 234-7131 ext. 0
(850) 234-7131 (fax)

The quaint Gulf View Motel resembles an inn. The two-story building has large apartments, with either a balcony or a porch, overlooking the Gulf. The efficiencies face the street.

- $/$$
- 21 Units
- Motel rooms; efficiencies with fully equipped kitchens; one- and two-bedroom apartments
- Pool
- Color Cable TV
- Guest Laundry
- Grills
- Shuffleboard
- Fax Services
- Mastercard, VISA, Discover, American Express
- Check-in: 2 P.M. Check-out: 11 A.M.

✿ Holiday Inn SunSpree Resort

11127 Front Beach Road
Panama City Beach, FL 32407
(850) 230-3400 ext. 414
(850) 235-0888 (fax)
(800) 633-0266 (Paradise Bound Resorts)

The Holiday Inn SunSpree Resort is a full-service hotel. All guest accommodations include either a king-size bed or two full-size beds, full-size refrigerator, coffee maker, hair dryer, and microwave. All rooms face the Gulf and have private balconies.

- TAC $$/$$$
- 340 Units
- Motel rooms and suites
- Pool
- Hot Tub
- Color Cable TV
- Guest Laundry
- Handicapped Access
- Restaurant/Bar
- Fitness Center
- Conference Facilities
- Fax Services
- Mastercard, VISA, Discover, American Express
- Check-in: 4 P.M. Check-out: 11 A.M.

✿ Holloway House

15405 Front Beach Road
Panama City Beach, FL 32413
(850) 234-6644
(850) 763-2852 (fax)
(800) 346-4709

Holloway House offers nicely decorated motel rooms and one- and two-bedroom apartments with full kitchens. The units feature private balconies that overlook the Gulf.

- TAC $$
- 100 Units
- Motel rooms; one- and two-bedroom apartments with fully equipped kitchens
- Pool
- Hot Tub
- Color Cable TV
- Guest Laundry
- Grills
- Handicapped Access
- Shuffleboard
- Fax Services
- Mastercard, VISA, Discover, American Express
- Check-in: 1 P.M. Check-out: 10 A.M.

Holiday Inn SunSpree Resort

🌀 Impala Motel

17751 Front Beach Road
Panama City Beach, FL 32413
(850) 234-6462
(800) 756-6462

A small, friendly motel, the Impala has rooms overlooking the pool and Gulf.

- $/$$
- 23 Units
- Motel rooms and efficiencies with fully equipped kitchens
- Pool
- Color Cable TV
- Grills
- Handicapped Access
- Shuffleboard
- Mastercard, VISA, Discover
- Check-in: 2 P.M. Check-out: 10 A.M.

☞ Miracle Strip Beach Motel

11827 Front Beach Road
Panama City Beach, FL 32407
(850) 234-3133
(850) 234-1233 (fax)
(800) 414-3963

The Miracle Strip Beach Motel is a newly remodeled, three-story motel located within walking distance of the Miracle Strip amusement and water parks.

- $$
- 52 Units
- Motel rooms, suites, and efficiencies with fully equipped kitchens
- Pool
- Color Cable TV
- Grills
- Fax Services
- Mastercard, VISA, Discover
- Check-in: 2 P.M. Check-out: 10 A.M.

☞ Moondrifter Condominiums

8815 Thomas Drive
Panama City Beach, FL 32408
(850) 234-9882
(850) 234-9786 (fax)
(800) 405-5048
email: moonrealty@aol.com

Moondrifter Condominiums are one- and two-bedroom luxury condominium units. All rooms feature two bathrooms, washer and dryer, and private balcony.

- $$
- 61 Units
- One- and two-bedroom condo-
  miniums
- Pool

- Color Cable TV
- Guest Laundry
- Fax Services
- Mastercard, VISA, Discover
- Check-in: 3 P.M. Check-out: 10 A.M.

⚉ Moonspinner Condominiums

4425 Thomas Drive
Panama City Beach, FL 32408
(850) 234-8900
(850) 233-0719 (fax)
(800) 223-3947

Moonspinner Condominiums are two- and three-bedroom family-oriented units. The building is adjacent to St. Andrews State Park, at the quiet end of Panama City Beach.

- $$$
- 121 Units
- Condominiums
- Pool
- Hot Tub
- Color Cable TV
- Grills

- Handicapped Access
- Shuffleboard
- Fitness Center
- Fax Services
- Mastercard, VISA
- Check-in: 3 P.M. Check-out: 11 A.M.

⚉ Oceanna Condos

8000 Surf Drive
Panama City Beach, FL 32408
(850) 234-9834
(800) 747-9834

The Oceanna is a family-oriented facility with units on the Gulf and economy-priced units across the street.

- $$
- 23 Units
- Condominiums
- Pool
- Color Cable TV
- Guest Laundry

- Grills
- Shuffleboard
- Mastercard, VISA, Discover
- Check-in: 2 P.M. Check-out: 10 A.M.

✍ Parson's Place

10719 Front Beach Road
Panama City Beach, FL 32407
(850) 234-2866
(850) 234-2866 (fax)
(800) 735-5605

Parson's Place has one-bedroom efficiencies with queen sleeper sofas. All units face the Gulf. Onsite washers and dryers are free to guests.

- $$
- 16 Units
- Efficiencies with fully equipped kitchens
- Color Cable TV
- Guest Laundry

- Grills
- Handicapped Access
- Pets (under 35 pounds; $100 deposit)
- Fax Services
- Mastercard, VISA
- Check-in: 2 P.M. Check-out: 10 A.M.

✍ Pineapple Beach Villas

19979 Front Beach Road
Panama City Beach, FL 32413
(850) 234-1788 ext. 300
(850) 234-1788 (fax)
(800) 234-1788

Pineapple Beach Villas has newly renovated one-, two- and three-bedroom condominiums, most with a beautiful view of the Gulf. Waverunner and scooter rentals are available.

- TAC $$/$$$
- 20 Units
- One-, two-, and three-bedroom condominiums
- Pool
- Hot Tub
- Color Cable TV
- Guest Laundry
- Grills

- Handicapped Access
- Restaurant/Bar
- Pets ($7.50 per day, maximum $25 per pet, per stay)
- Fax Services
- Mastercard, VISA, Discover, American Express
- Check-in: 3 P.M. Check-out: 10 A.M.

Port of Call Motel

15817 Front Beach Road
Panama City Beach, FL 32413
(850) 234-6666
(850) 234-2601 (fax)
(800) 659-1213

All units at the Port of Call face the Gulf. Two restaurants are located directly across the street.

- TAC $$
- 157 Units
- Motel rooms, suites, and efficiencies with fully equipped kitchens
- Pool
- Color Cable TV
- Handicapped Access
- Fax Services
- Mastercard, VISA, Discover, American Express
- Check-in: 2 P.M. Check-out: 10 A.M.

Ramada Inn Beach

12907 Front Beach Road
Panama City Beach, FL 32407
(850) 230-3400 ext. 414
(850) 235-0888 (fax)
(800) 633-0266 (Paradise Bound Resorts)

Ramada Inn Beach is a full-service resort hotel. All rooms are tropically decorated and are oceanfront with private balconies.

- TAC $$/$$$
- 147 Units
- Motel rooms and suites
- Pool
- Hot Tub
- Color Cable TV
- Guest Laundry
- Grills
- Restaurant/Bar
- Fitness Center
- Conference Facilities
- Fax Services
- Mastercard, VISA
- Check-in: 4 P.M. Check-out: 11 A.M.

✍ Sandpiper-Beacon

17403 Front Beach Road
Panama City Beach, FL 32413
(850) 234-2154
(850) 233-0278 (fax)
(800) 488-8828
http://www.sandpiperbeacon.com

The Sandpiper-Beacon is a beautiful resort with two outdoor swimming pools, one enclosed heated pool, and a huge beachfront hot tub.

- TAC $
- 154 Units
- Motel rooms; suites; one- and two-bedroom apartments with fully equipped kitchens
- Pool
- Hot Tub
- Color Cable TV
- Guest Laundry
- Grills
- Shuffleboard
- Pets (under 10 pounds; $50 deposit)
- Conference Facilities
- Fax Services
- Mastercard, VISA, Discover, American Express
- Check-in: 4 P.M. Check-out: 9 A.M.

✍ Sea Star Inn

900 Gulfside Drive
Panama City Beach, FL 32407
(850) 234-9195
(800) 972-3759

The Sea Star Inn is a family owned and operated motel providing "down home hospitality" to those who like a friendly casual atmosphere. The super clean rooms have balconies overlooking the pool and beach.

- $$
- 20 Units
- Motel rooms and efficiencies with fully equipped kitchens
- Pool
- Color Cable TV
- Mastercard, VISA, Discover
- Check-in: 1 P.M. Check-out: 10 A.M.

⟨⟨⟩ Sea Witch Motel

21905 Front Beach Road
Panama City Beach, FL 32413
(850) 234-5722
(850) 233-4971 (fax)
(800) 322-4571

Designed for family fun on the Gulf, the Sea Witch has one- and two-bedroom efficiencies, single and double motel rooms, and suites.

- $/$$
- 20 Units
- Motel rooms; suites; one- and two-bedroom efficiencies with fully equipped kitchens
- Pool
- Color Cable TV
- Guest Laundry
- Grills
- Shuffleboard
- Conference facilities
- Fax Services
- Mastercard, VISA, Discover, American Express
- Check-in: 3 P.M. Check-out: 11 A.M.

Sea Witch Motel

☞ Sky Way Motel

16801 Front Beach Road
Panama City Beach, FL 32413
(850) 234-8851
(800) 887-4879

The newly renovated Sky Way Motel has rooms with private balconies overlooking the Gulf. It is a small, clean motel featuring a large, Gulf-side pool and easy access to all
beach attractions.

- $$
- 36 Units
- Motel rooms; one- and two-bedroom apartments with fully equipped kitchens
- Pool
- Hot Tub
- Color Cable TV
- Grills
- Shuffleboard
- Mastercard, VISA, Discover, American Express
- Check-in: 2 P.M. Check-out: 11 A.M.

☞ Sting Ray Condos

8001 Surf Drive
Panama City Beach, FL 32408
(850) 234-2060
(850) 230-5422 (fax)
(800) 426-1455

The Sting Ray offers rooms for one to six persons. Located in a quiet area, it caters primarily to families. Most units are Gulf-front.

- $$
- 18 Units
- Condominiums
- Pool
- Color Cable TV
- Guest Laundry
- Grills
- Mastercard, VISA, Discover
- Check-in: 2 P.M. Check-out: 10 A.M.

☞ Sugar Beach Motel

16819 Front Beach Road
Panama City Beach, FL 32413

(850) 234-2142
(850) 785-3444 (fax)
(800) 528-1273

The Sugar Beach Motel is a family-oriented motel with newly renovated one- and two- bedroom apartments.

- $/$$
- 106 Units
- Motel rooms; one- and two-bedroom apartments
- Pool
- Hot Tub
- Color Cable TV

- Guest Laundry
- Grills
- Handicapped Facilities
- Shuffleboard
- Mastercard, VISA, Discover, American Express
- Check-in: 2 P.M. Check-out: 10 A.M.

෴ Sunset Inn

8109 Surf Drive
Panama City Beach, FL 32408
(850) 234-7370
(850) 234-7370 ext. 303 (fax)

The Sunset Inn offers beautiful one- and two-bedroom rooms with kitchens overlooking the Gulf or pool. Nestled among sandy white dunes, the inn offers a quiet place to vacation, yet it is still close to area attractions and restaurants.

- $$
- 50 Units
- Motel rooms, suites, and efficiencies with fully equipped kitchens
- Pool
- Color Cable TV

- Guest Laundry
- Grills
- Fax Services
- Mastercard, VISA, Discover, American Express
- Check-in: 2 P.M. Check-out: 10 A.M.

෴ Wind Drift Motel

14521 Front Beach Road
Panama City Beach, FL 32407
(850) 234-2415 ext. 100
(888) 280-3434
http://www.travelbase.com/destination/panama-city/wind-drift/

All units at the Wind Drift Motel have two double beds, kitchens, and private balconies.

- $$
- 40 Units
- Efficiencies with fully equipped kitchens
- Pool
- Color Cable TV

- Handicapped Access
- Pets (prefer small pets, $25 per stay)
- Mastercard, VISA, Discover, American Express
- Check-in: 1 P.M. Check-out: 11 A.M.

Resort Rental Companies

St. Andrew Bay Resort Management, Inc.
Panama City Beach
(850) 235-4075
(850) 233-2833 (fax)
(800) 621-2462
http://www.sabre1.net

Points of Interest

St. Andrews State Recreation Area
4415 Thomas Drive
Panama City Beach, FL 32408
(850) 233-5140
Campsites, fishing, hiking trails, concessions, swimming, guided tours

Gulf World
15412 Front Beach Road
Panama City Beach, FL 32413
(850) 234-5271
Features tropical gardens and shows including dolphins, sea lions, parrots, and scuba divers
Hours: 9 A.M. to 3 P.M.
Admission: Adults, $13.95; children ages 5 to 12, $7.95; children 4 and under, free

Miracle Strip Amusement Park
12000 West Front Beach Road
Panama City Beach, FL 32407
(850) 234-5810
(800) 538-7395
A family-oriented amusement park featuring twenty-seven rides and attractions, live shows, and arcade games
Hours: Seasonal; call for hours
Admission: Adults and children, $16

Shipwreck Island Water Park
12000 Front Beach Road
Panama City Beach, FL 32407
(850) 234-0368
(800) 538-7395
A water theme park featuring rides, games, children's area, and sun decks
Hours: Seasonal; call for hours
Admission: Taller than 50 inches, $18; shorter than 50 inches, $15

Zooworld, A Zoological and Botanical Garden
9008 Front Beach Road
Panama City Beach, FL 32407
(850) 230-1243
More than 300 species of plants and animals from around the world are exhibited here. Also features a petting zoo with a giraffe feeding platform
Hours: 9 A.M. to dusk, daily
Admission: Adults, $8.95; children ages 3 to 11, $6.50; children 2 and under, free

Dining Out

Captain Anderson's Restaurant
5551 North Lagoon Drive
Panama City Beach
(850) 234-2225

Hours: 4 P.M. to 10 P.M.; closed Sunday
Features: fresh seafood, children's menu; casual dress; dine early and watch the fishing fleets come in (between 4:30 and 5 P.M.)
Dinner: $10.95 to $34.95

Hamilton's Seafood Restaurant
5711 North Lagoon Drive
Panama City Beach
(850) 234-1255
Hours: 4 P.M. to 10 P.M. (summer); 5 P.M. to 10 P.M. (winter)
Features: seafood, steak, pasta, homemade desserts, children's menu, daily specials; casual waterfront dining
Dinner: $10.95 to $27.95

The Sunset Restaurant
12405 Front Beach Road
Panama City Beach
(850) 234-7683
Hours: 4 P.M. to 10 P.M.
Features: seafood, steak, seafood buffet, children's menu; casual beachfront dining
Dinner: $6.99 to $29.99

Mexico Beach

Accommodations

☞ Driftwood Inn

2105 Highway 98
Mexico Beach, FL 32410
(850) 648-5126
(850) 648-8505

The Driftwood Inn offers quaint one- and two-bedroom cottages.

- $$
- 25 Units
- Efficiencies with fully
  equipped kitchens; one- and
  two-bedroom cottages
- Color Cable TV
- Guest Laundry

- Grills
- Handicapped Access
- Pets (no fees or deposits)
- Fax Services
- Mastercard, VISA, Discover,
  American Express
- Check-in: 1 P.M. Check-out: 11 A.M.

☞ El Governor Motel

1701 US Highway 98
Mexico Beach, FL 32410
(850) 648-5757
(850) 648-5754 (fax)

The El Governor offers spacious rooms that feature king-size or double beds and private balconies overlooking the Gulf.

- TAC $$
- 123 Units
- Motel rooms and efficiencies
  with fully equipped kitchens
- Pool
- Color Cable TV
- Guest Laundry
- Grills

- Handicapped Access
- Bar
- Conference Facilities
- Fax Services
- Mastercard, VISA, Discover,
  American Express
- Check-in: 2 P.M. Check-out: 11 A.M.

✆ Sandman Motel

2303 Highway 98
Mexico Beach, FL 32410
(850) 648-5200
(850) 648-8244 (fax)

The family owned and operated Sandman Motel is a one-story building made of cypress wood offering one- and two-bedroom units with queen beds.

- $$
- 8 Units
- Motel rooms; efficiencies with fully equipped kitchens; and condominiums
- Color Cable TV
- Grills
- Handicapped Access
- Pets (small pets preferred; $10 per stay)
- Fax Services
- Mastercard, VISA, Discover, American Express
- Check-in: 1 P.M. Check-out: 11 A.M.

✆ Surfside Inn

118 38th Street
Mexico Beach, FL 32410
(850) 648-5771
(850) 648-5772 (fax)

The Surfside Inn offers a relaxing place to spend a night, a weekend, or a winter season. It is a small, family-oriented motel.

- TAC $$
- 12 Units
- Motel rooms and one-bedroom apartments with fully equipped kitchens
- Color Cable TV
- Grills
- Fax Services
- Mastercard, VISA, Discover
- Check-in: 1 P.M. Check-out: 11 A.M.

Dining Out

Fish House Restaurant & Lounge
3006 Highway 98
Mexico Beach
(850) 648-8950
Hours: 11 A.M. to 9 P.M.
Features: fresh seafood, steak, specialty dishes, children's menu; casual dress
Lunch: $4.95 to $12.95
Dinner: $4.95 to $12.95

Sharon's Cafe
1100 Highway 98
Mexico Beach
(850) 648-8634
Hours: 5 A.M. to 2 P.M.
Features: breakfast served anytime; world-famous Western hash-browns and smiley-face pancakes; casual dining
Breakfast: $1.25 to $5.95
Lunch: $2.50 to $4.25

St. George Island

Accommodations

✆ Buccaneer Inn

160 West Gorrie Drive
St. George Island, FL 32328
(850) 927-2585
(850) 927-3266 (fax)
(800) 847-2091

The Buccaneer Inn features Gulf-front and poolside rooms and efficiencies. All efficiency units are complete with a fully equipped kitchen and all the comforts of home. This is the only motel on the beach in St. George.

- $$
- 92 Units
- Motel rooms and efficiencies
  with fully equipped kitchens
- Pool
- Color Cable TV

- Handicapped Access
- Conference Facilities
- Fax Services
- Mastercard, VISA
- Check-in: 2 P.M. Check-out: 11 A.M.

Resort Rental Companies

Collins Vacation Rentals, Inc.
St. George Island
(800) 423-7418

Sun Coast Realty
St. George Island
(800) 341-2021

Dining Out

Apalachicola Seafood Grill & Steak House
100 Market Street
Apalachicola (9.5 miles from St. George Island)
(850) 653-9510
Hours: 11:30 A.M. to 9 P.M.
Features: local fried and grilled seafood, world's largest fried fish sandwich, daily specials, homemade soups, children's menu; casual dress
Lunch: $3.50 to $14.95
Dinner: $3.50 to $14.95

Blue Parrot Oyster Bar & Grill
216 West Gorrie Drive
St. George Island
(850) 927-2987
Hours: 11 A.M. to 10 P.M.
Features: oysters, fresh seafood, conch fritters, children's menu; air conditioned dining by the Gulf of Mexico; beachside tiki bar
Lunch: $4.95 to $7.95
Dinner: $10.95 to $21.95

Caroline's Riverfront
123 Water Street
Apalachicola (9 miles from St. George Island)
(850) 653-8139
Hours: 8 A.M. to 10 P.M.
Features: fresh seafood, steak, homemade gumbo, children's menu; upscale dining in a casual riverfront setting
Lunch: $5.95 to $10.95
Dinner: $10.95 to $26.95

Happy Pelican
49 West Pine Street
St. George Island
(850) 927-9826

Hours: 7 A.M. to 12 A.M.

Features: breakfast served daily; seafood, steak, pasta, homemade soups; casual dining; friendly service

Lunch: $2.95 to $8.95

Dinner: $8.95 to $14.95

PANHANDLE AREA GOLF
(Semi-private and Public)

Bay Point Yacht & Country Club
100 Delwood Beach Road
Panama City Beach
(850) 235-6950
Semi-private; driving range

Club at Hidden Creek
3070 PGA Boulevard
Navarre
(850) 939-4604
Semi-private; driving range, restaurant

Club at Sandy Creek
1732 Highway 2297
Panama City
(850) 871-2673
Semi-private; driving range

Eglin AFB Golf Course
1527 Fairway Drive
Niceville
(850) 882-2949
Public

Emerald Bay Plantation
40001 Emerald Coast Highway
Destin
(850) 837-5197
Semi-private; driving range, restaurant

Holiday Golf & Racquet Club
100 Fairway Boulevard
Panama City Beach

(850) 234-1800
Semi-private; driving range, restaurant

Hombre Golf Club
120 Coyote Pass
Panama City Beach
(850) 234-3673
Semi-private; driving range, restaurant

Indian Bayou Golf & Country Club
Airport Road
Destin
(850) 837-6191
Semi-private; driving range, restaurant

Island Golf Center
1306 Miracle Strip Parkway
Fort Walton Beach
(850) 244-1612
Semi-private

Majette Dunes Golf & Country Club
5304 Majette Tower Road
Panama City
(850) 769-4740
Semi-private; driving range, restaurant

Osceola/City Municipal Golf Course
300 Tonawanda Drive
Pensacola
(850) 456-2761
Public; restaurant

Perdido Bay Resort
One Doug Ford Drive
Pensacola
(850) 492-1223
Public; driving range, restaurant

Saint Josephs Bay Country Club
RC 30 South
Port St. Joe
(850) 227-1751
Semi-private; driving range, restaurant

Sandestin Resort Golf Course
5500 Highway 98 East
Destin
(850) 267-8155
Semi-private; driving range, restaurant

Sandpiper Cove Golf Course
off US Highway 98
Destin
(850) 837-9121
Semi-private

Santa Rosa Golf & Beach Club
Highway 30A
Santa Rosa Beach

(850) 267-2229
Semi-private; driving range, restaurant

Saufley Golf Course
2423 Saufley Road
Pensacola
(850) 452-1097
Semi-private

Scenic Hills Country Club
8891 Burning Tree Road
Pensacola
(850) 476-0611
Semi-private; driving range, restaurant

Seascape Golf & Racquet Club
100 Seascape Drive
Destin
(850) 837-9181
Public; driving range, restaurant

Signal Hill Golf Course
9615 Thomas Drive
Panama City
(850) 234-5051
Public; restaurant

CHAMBERS OF COMMERCE

Destin Chamber of Commerce
1021 Highway 98
Destin, FL 32541
(850) 837-6241

Greater Fort Walton Beach Chamber of Commerce
34 Miracle Strip Parkway, South East
Fort Walton Beach, FL 32549
(850) 244-8191

Mexico Beach Chamber of Commerce
PO Box 13382

Mexico Beach, FL 32410
(850) 648-8196

Panama City Beaches Chamber of Commerce
PO Box 9348
Panama City Beach, FL 32407
(850) 235-1159

Pensacola Area Chamber of Commerce
PO Box 550
Pensacola, FL 32593
(850) 438-4081

Suncoast Beaches

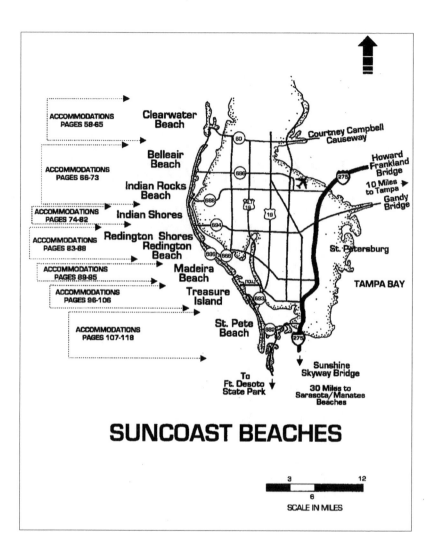

SUNCOAST BEACHES

ACCOMMODATIONS PAGES 58-65

ACCOMMODATIONS PAGES 66-73

ACCOMMODATIONS PAGES 74-82

ACCOMMODATIONS PAGES 83-88

ACCOMMODATIONS PAGES 89-95

ACCOMMODATIONS PAGES 96-106

ACCOMMODATIONS PAGES 107-118

Clearwater Beach

Belleair Beach

Indian Rocks Beach

Indian Shores

Redington Shores
Redington Beach

Madeira Beach

Treasure Island

St. Pete Beach

To
Ft. Desoto
State Park

Courtney Campbell Causeway

Howard Frankland Bridge

10 Miles to Tampa

Gandy Bridge

St. Petersburg

TAMPA BAY

Sunshine Skyway Bridge

30 Miles to Sarasota/Manatee Beaches

60

688

ALT 19

19

694

699

688

693

682

275

275

SCALE IN MILES

3   12
6

Overview

*T*he Suncoast region of Florida offers many beautiful beach areas. Its convenient location to Tampa and Orlando is also appealing to travelers taking day trips to either city and visiting the major theme parks each has to offer.

Clearwater Beach, with its beachfront hotels, is the northernmost beach community that you will encounter in the West Central area. Offering a variety of activities including beach volleyball, watercraft rentals, parasailing, and scuba diving, Clearwater Beach is a popular destination for many vacationers. The south end of the beach tends to be more populated since this is where the majority of hotels, city fishing pier, and marina are located. If you prefer a more private beach, take a walk up to the north end, which is more residential. You won't have any trouble finding restaurants or shopping: the area offers plenty of both.

Sand Key is located just over the Clearwater Pass Bridge from Clearwater Beach. Here you will find many high-rise condominiums with only one hotel located on the beach. A sidewalk runs down Gulf Boulevard, making a nice pathway for rollerblading or bicycling.

If you are looking for a secluded spot, you will find it along the twelve-mile stretch between Belleair and Madeira beaches, including Indian Rocks Beach, Indian Shores, Redington Beach, and Redington Shores. Most of the accommodations in this area have their own private beaches. Many are quaint motels, "throwbacks" to the 1940s and 1950s.

Madeira Beach has two public beach areas with metered parking and activities such as beach volleyball, watercraft rentals, and parasailing. John's Pass Village and Boardwalk, located at John's Pass Bridge, provides an array of unique shops and restaurants in a scenic setting. Deep-sea fishing trips, sunset cruises, and casino cruises all originate there.

Treasure Island boasts the widest beach on the Suncoast (three and a half miles). The beaches on Treasure Island are all public; metered parking is available at the Treasure Island Municipal Beach. This facility offers concessions, restrooms, showers, and volleyball nets. Watercraft rentals and parasailing are also available. A wide assortment of shops and restaurants is located along Gulf Boulevard.

St. Pete Beach offers miles of beaches and an abundance of Gulf-front accommodations. This is the home of the Don Cesar, known as the"Pink Palace," a historic landmark for this area. You will also find hundreds of shops and restaurants to fit your needs.

Climate

(Temperature by Degrees Farenheight)

Season	Average Low	Average High	Gulf Water
January–March	50	76	60s–70s
April–June	62	90	70s–80s
July–September	73	90	80s
October–December	51	84	70s–80s

Getting There

By Air

Tampa International Airport
(813) 870-8700
Location: Five miles west of downtown Tampa (approximately 30 to 35 minutes' driving time to most Suncoast beach area destinations)

St. Petersburg–Clearwater International Airport
(813) 531-1451

Location: Seven miles southeast of Clearwater (approximately 20 minutes' driving time to most Suncoast beach area destinations)

By Car

INTERSTATE 75: Follow signs from I-75 south to I-275 heading into Tampa. To access Clearwater Beach and Sand Key, take Exit 20 and follow signs for SR 60 West via the Courtney Campbell Causeway. To reach the lower Pinellas Suncoast beaches, continue to follow I-275 south and west across the Howard Frankland Bridge. Take Exit 18 West for Indian Rocks Beach, Exit 15 for Redington Beach, Exit 11 for Treasure Island and Madeira Beach, and Exit 5 (the Bayway) for St. Pete Beach.

INTERSTATE 95: Take I-95 to I-4 West towards Orlando and Tampa. At the I-4/I-275 interchange, follow signs for I-275 South.

Clearwater Beach

Accommodations

☞ Adam's Mark Caribbean Gulf Resort

430 South Gulfview Boulevard
Clearwater Beach, FL 34630
(813) 443-5714

Conveniently located overlooking Clearwater Pass and Beach, this high-rise resort is a hub for live entertainment and special events, including an excellent Sunday brunch.

- $$$
- 207 Units
- Hotel rooms and suites
- Pool
- Hot Tub
- Restaurant/Lounge

- Conference Facilities
- Fax Services
- Mastercard, VISA, Discover, American Express
- Check-in: 4 P.M. Check-out: 11 A.M.

Adam's Mark Caribbean Gulf Resort

☜ Clearwater Beach Garden Apartment Motel

14 Somerset Street
Clearwater Beach, FL 34630
(813) 442-8874

These quaint, lushly landscaped tropical garden units provide an intimate setting in which to relax and enjoy the sights and sounds of the beach.

- TAC $
- 9 Units
- One- and two-bedroom efficiencies with fully equipped kitchens
- Pool
- Color Cable TV
- Guest Laundry
- Grills
- Shuffleboard
- Mastercard, VISA, Discover
- Check-in: 2 P.M. Check-out: 10 A.M.

☜ Clearwater Beach Hotel

500 Mandalay Avenue
Clearwater Beach, FL 34630
(813) 441-2425
(813) 449-2083 (fax)
(800) 292-2295

The Clearwater Beach Hotel is a traditional, grand, old, Southern-style hotel with rooms that have beautiful vistas of the Gulf or Clearwater Harbor.

- TAC $$$
- 150 Units
- Hotel rooms; suites; one- and two-bedroom apartments with fully equipped kitchens
- Pool
- Color Cable TV
- Guest Laundry
- Grills
- Handicapped Access
- Restaurant/Bar
- Shuffleboard
- Pets (under 20 pounds; in designated rooms)
- Conference Facilities
- Fax Services
- Mastercard, VISA, American Express
- Check-in: 3 P.M. Check-out: 12 P.M.

Clearwater Beach Hotel

☞ Flamingo Beachfront Suites

450 North Gulfview Boulevard
Clearwater Beach, FL 34630
(813) 441-8019
(813) 446-6599 (fax)
(800) 821-8019
http://www.clearwaterbeach.com/flamingo/flamingo.html

The Flamingo Beachfront Suites are located on 287 feet of private beach and are centrally located, within walking distance of shops, restaurants, Pier 60, and the city marina.

- TAC $$
- 55 Units
- Suites and efficiencies with fully equipped kitchens
- Pool
- Hot Tub
- Color Cable TV
- Guest Laundry
- Grills
- Shuffleboard
- Fitness Center
- Fax services
- Mastercard, VISA, Discover
- Check-in: 3 P.M. Check-out: 10 A.M.

⌘ The Haddon House Inn

14 Idlewild Street
Clearwater Beach, FL 34630
(813) 461-2914
(813) 461-2914 ext. 121 (fax)
http://www.internet-ad.com/haddon/

The oldest house on the island, Haddon House offers rooms with red pine floors, most with a Gulf view. It is located in a quiet residential area.

- TAC $/$$
- 14 Units
- One- and two-bedroom apartments with fully equipped kitchens
- Pool
- Color Cable TV
- Grills
- Guest Laundry
- Fax services
- Mastercard, VISA, Discover, American Express
- Check-in: 2 P.M. Check-out: 10 A.M.

The Haddon House Inn

❧ The Patio Motel

15 Somerset Street
Clearwater Beach, FL 34630
(813) 442-1862
(813) 447-5825 (fax)

The Patio Motel, nestled on North Clearwater Beach, is famous for its warm, casual atmosphere. The quiet, comfortable apartments are immaculately clean. Beachfront porches and balconies provide nice views of the Gulf.

- $
- 14 Units
- Motel rooms; efficiencies; one- and two-bedroom apartments with fully equipped kitchens
- Color Cable TV
- Guest Laundry
- Grills
- Fax Services
- Mastercard, VISA
- Check-in: 2 P.M. Check-out: 10 A.M.

The Patio Motel

Sheraton Sand Key Resort

✍ **Sheraton Sand Key Resort**

1160 Gulf Boulevard
Clearwater Beach, FL 34630
(813) 593-6001
(813) 593-6004 (fax)

The Sheraton Sand Key is a beautifully landscaped high-rise, located on one of America's top fifteen beaches. It is the only hotel located on the beach on Sand Key.

- TAC $$
- 390 Units
- Hotel rooms and suites
- Pool
- Hot Tub
- Color Cable TV
- Handicapped Access
- Restaurant/Bar
- Fitness Center
- Conference Facilities
- Fax Services
- Mastercard, VISA, Discover, American Express
- Check-in: 3 P.M. Check-out: 11 A.M.

Points of Interest

Clearwater Ferry Service
Clearwater Beach Marina
25 Causeway Boulevard
Clearwater Beach, FL 33767
(813) 442-7433
One-and-three-quarter-hour dolphin encounter cruise.
Hours: Call for cruise schedule
Admission: Adults, $10; children ages 12 and under, $5.75

Clearwater Marine Aquarium
249 Windward Passage (Island Estates)
Clearwater Beach, FL 33767
(813) 447-0980
A center dedicated to the rescue and rehabilitation of marine life
Hours: Monday-Friday, 9 A.M. to 5 P.M.; Saturday, 9 A.M. to 4 P.M.;
Sunday, 11 A.M. to 4 P.M.
Admission: Adults, $6.75; children ages 4 to 12, $4.25; children 3 and
under, free

Pier 60 (located just south of the Doubletree Resort on Clearwater Beach)
Fishing: (813) 462-6466
Open 24 hours for pier fishing; fishing licenses not required; rod
rentals available; full bait shop and snack bar
A year-round street festival featuring local artists, crafters, and
performers; Thursday through Monday, two hours before and after
sunset
Admission: Adults, $5.35; seniors, $4.45; children ages 10 to 16, $3.75;
children under 10, $2.50 Sunsets: (813) 449-1036

Sand Key Park
1060 Gulf Boulevard
Clearwater Beach, FL 33767
(813) 595-7677
Sand Key Park, located directly on the Gulf of Mexico, is a Pinellas
County park offering showers, restrooms, picnic tables, and a play-

ground. Dogs on leashes are permitted in the park but not on the beach.

Hours: 7 A.M. to dark

Admission: Free; parking spaces are metered ($.75 per hour; quarters only)

Dining Out

Frenchy's Saltwater Cafe
419 Poinsettia Avenue
Clearwater Beach
(813) 461-6295
Hours: 11 A.M. to 11 P.M.; Sunday, 12 P.M. to 11 P.M.
Features: many menu choices; casual dress; just a few blocks from the beach
Lunch: $5 to $16
Dinner: $5 to $16

Seafood & Sunsets
351 South Gulfview Boulevard
Clearwater Beach
(813) 441-2548
Hours: 11 A.M. to 10 P.M.
Features: seafood, steak, sandwiches; casual dress; across the street from the beach
Lunch: $3.95 to $21
Dinner: $3.95 to $21

Shepard's
601 South Gulfview Boulevard
Clearwater Beach
(813) 441-6875
Hours: 8 A.M. to 11 A.M.; 11:30 A.M. to 3 P.M.; 4 P.M. to 10 P.M.
Features: Sunday brunch; casual dress; outside dining overlooking water; entertainment
Lunch: $4 to $7
Dinner: $5 to $19

Belleair Beach and Indian Rocks Beach

Accommodations

☞ Alpaugh's Gulf Beach Motel Apartments

68 Gulf Boulevard
Indian Rocks Beach, FL 33785
(813) 595-2589

Alpaugh's has two two-story buildings with rooms that open up to a courtyard. The motel is located across the road from the Intracoastal Waterway and has a private fishing pier.

- $$
- 16 Units
- One-bedroom apartments with fully equipped kitchens
- Color Cable TV

- Guest Laundry
- Grills
- Handicapped Access
- Mastercard, VISA, Discover
- Check-in: 2 P.M. Check-out: 10 A.M.

Alpaugh's Gulf Beach Motel Apartments

☞ Anchor Court Apartments & Motel

940 Gulf Boulevard North
Indian Rocks Beach, FL 33785
(813) 595-4449

This two-story apartment/motel has 150 feet of beautiful beach. All apartments are clean and newly carpeted.

- $/$$
- 20 Units
- Motel rooms; one- and two-bedroom apartments with fully equipped kitchens
- Pool
- Color Cable TV
- Guest Laundry
- Grills
- Handicapped Access
- Shuffleboard
- Mastercard, VISA, Discover, American Express
- Check-in: 2 P.M. Check-out: 10 A.M.

Anchor Court Apartment & Motel

☞ Belleair Beach Resort Motel

2040 Gulf Boulevard
Belleair Beach, FL 33786
(813) 595-1696
(813) 593-5433 (fax)

(800) 780-1696

http://www.belleairbeachresort.com

This resort is privately owned and operated. It is well-kept with many units recently renovated.

- $$
- 43 Units
- Motel rooms; one- and two-bedroom apartments with fully equipped kitchens
- Pool
- Color Cable TV
- Guest Laundry
- Grills
- Shuffleboard
- Fax Services
- Mastercard, VISA, Discover, American Express
- Check-in: 2 P.M. Check-out: 11 A.M.

☞ Fifty Gulfside Condominiums

50 Gulf Boulevard
Indian Rocks Beach, FL 33785
(813) 595-6739
(813) 596-1966 (fax)

This one-, two- and three-bedroom condominium complex offers units with private balconies facing either the Gulf or Intracoastal Waterway. There is a five-night minimum stay required.

- TAC $$
- 54 Units
- Condominiums
- Pool
- Color Cable TV
- Guest Laundry
- Grills
- Handicapped Access
- Fax Services
- Mastercard, VISA, Discover
- Check-in: 2 P.M. Check-out: 10 A.M.

☞ The Happy Fiddler Condominiums

60 Gulf Boulevard
Indian Rocks Beach, FL 33785
(813) 595-8966
(813) 595-8966 (fax)

All units at the Happy Fiddler Condominiums face the Gulf and are fully equipped. Enjoy watching the sunset from your private balcony.

The Happy Fiddler Condominiums

- $$$
- 28 Units
- Condominiums
- Pool
- Color Cable TV

- Guest Laundry
- Grills
- No Credit Cards
- Check-in: 2 P.M. Check-out: 10 A.M.

☙ Hidden Cove Motel Apartments

36 Gulf Boulevard
Indian Rocks Beach, FL 33785
(813) 595-3905

Hidden Cove is a privately owned and operated motel offering clean and tastefully furnished apartments. Relax on the terrace under tiki huts overlooking the beach.

- TAC $/$$
- 14 Units
- Efficiencies; one- and two-bed-room apartments with fully equipped kitchens
- Color Cable TV

- Guest Laundry
- Grills
- Shuffleboard
- No Credit Cards
- Check-in: 2 P.M. Check-out: 10 A.M.

✈ Nautical Watch Beach Resort

3420 Gulf Boulevard
Belleair Beach, FL 34635
(813) 595-4747

The Nautical Watch has twenty-one luxurious apartments with a casual, friendly atmosphere. The two-bedroom units can accommodate up to six people.

- $$
- 21 Units
- One- and two-bedroom apartments with fully equipped kitchens
- Pool
- Hot Tub

- Color Cable TV
- Guest Laundry
- Grills
- Shuffleboard
- Mastercard, VISA, Discover, American Express
- Check-in: 3 P.M. Check-out: 10 A.M.

✈ Pelican West

108 21st Avenue
Indian Rocks Beach, FL 33785
(813) 595-9741

Pelican West has four one-bedroom apartments that are neatly furnished for a comfortable stay at the beach. Cleanliness and friendliness are Pelican West's greatest assets. Their goal is to keep rates low so that everyone can enjoy a beach vacation.

- TAC $
- 4 Units
- Motel rooms; one-bedroom apartments with fully equipped kitchens
- Color Cable TV

- Grills
- Handicapped Access
- Mastercard, VISA
- Check-in: 2 P.M. Check-out: 10:30 A.M.

✈ Sandy Shores Motel & Apartments

816 Gulf Boulevard
Indian Rocks Beach, FL 33785
(813) 595-3226
(813) 595-3226 ext. 315 (fax)

Sandy Shores has charming apartment efficiencies and cottages that provide a romantic getaway for two, a comfortable family vacation, or a relaxing escape.

- $/$$
- 12 Units
- One- and two-bedroom apartments with fully equipped kitchens; cottages
- Pool
- Color Cable TV
- Guest Laundry
- Grills
- Pets ($10 per stay)
- Fax Services
- Mastercard, VISA, Discover
- Check-in: 1 P.M. Check-out: 10 A.M.

ॐ Sea Gem Cottages & Apartments
One 23rd Avenue
Indian Rocks Beach, FL 33785
(813) 595-2017

Quaint, family-owned Sea Gem Cottages have been preserved in the "old Florida" style.

- $$
- 7 Units
- One-bedroom apartments with fully equipped kitchens; two-bedroom cottages
- Color Cable TV
- Grills
- Restaurant
- No credit cards
- Check-in: 2 P.M. Check-out: 10 A.M.

ॐ Sol-Y-Mar Cottages
1306 Gulf Boulevard
Indian Rocks Beach, FL 33785
(813) 595-3010

Sol-Y-Mar has one- and two-bedroom cottages that sleep five people and are rustic and comfortable. Restaurants and bars are located across the street.

- $
- 2 Units
- Cottages
- Color Cable TV
- No Credit Cards
- Check-in: 2 P.M. Check-out: 11 A.M.

Sol-Y-Mar Cottages

Whispering Waters Beach Castle Apartments
604 Gulf Boulevard
Indian Rocks Beach, FL 33785
(813) 595-4505

Whispering Waters offers efficiencies and one- and two-bedroom apartments in four separate, well-kept buildings. Some of the units include a balcony overlooking the Gulf.

- $$
- 20 Units
- Efficiencies; one- and two-bed-room apartments with fully equipped kitchens
- Pool
- Color Cable TV
- Guest Laundry
- Grills
- Shuffleboard
- Mastercard, VISA, Discover, American Express
- Check-in: 2 P.M. Check-out: 10 A.M.

Whispering Waters Beach Castle Apartments

Dining Out

2721 Surfside
2721 Gulf Boulevard
Indian Rocks
(813) 595-7877
Hours: 12 P.M. to 2 A.M.
Features: seafood, steak, pasta, sandwiches; casual dress
Lunch: $2.95 to $6.95
Dinner: $8.95 to $22.95

Guppy's on the Beach
1701 North Gulf Boulevard
Indian Rocks
(813) 593-2032
Hours: 11:30 A.M. to 10:30 P.M.; Friday and Saturday until 11 P.M.
Features: seafood, steak, sandwiches; patio dining available; casual dress
Lunch: $8 to $20
Dinner: $8 to $20

Indian Shores

Accommodations

☙ B & B Cottages
19538 Gulf Boulevard
Indian Shores, FL 33785
(813) 595-6520

These one-bedroom efficiency cottages are no further than 50 feet from the beach and sleep four to six people.

- $
- 6 Units
- Efficiencies with fully equipped kitchens
- Color Cable TV
- Grills
- Shuffleboard
- No credit cards
- Check-in: 2 P.M. Check-out: 10:30 A.M.

☙ Beach Side Suites
19218 Gulf Boulevard
Indian Shores, FL 33785
(813) 595-7635
(813) 595-4450 (fax)
(800) 779-7999

Many rooms at the Beach Side Suites have their own two-person Jacuzzi, perfect for a honeymoon or special occasion. The two-story buildings are clean and well-maintained.

- TAC $$
- 20 Units
- Suites; one- and two-bedroom apartments with fully equipped kitchens
- Pool
- Hot Tub (in room)
- Color Cable TV
- Guest Laundry
- Handicapped Access (limited)
- Fax Services
- Mastercard, VISA, Discover, American Express
- Check-in: 2 P.M. Check-out: 11 A.M.

Beach Side Suites

⚭ Casa Chica Cottages

19000 Gulf Boulevard
Indian Shores, FL 33785
(813) 596-1602
(813) 596-0538 (fax)
(800) 562-5335
http://www.clearwaterfl.com/mall/casa

Casa Chica, a new member of Florida's Superior Small Lodgings, offers four beachside cottages with privacy and quiet. Ken and Galina live on the premises and have been the owners since 1979. The heated swim/spa and bricked, Spanish-style courtyard give the Casa Chica a unique ambiance.

- TAC $$
- 4 Units
- Cottages with fully equipped kitchens
- Pool
- Hot Tub
- Color Cable TV
- Grills
- Handicapped Access
- Pets (fee ranges from $15 to $35 depending on pet)
- Fax Services
- No Credit Cards
- Check-in: 2:30 P.M. Check-out: 10 A.M.

Casa Chica Cottages

Edgewater Beach Resort

☞ Edgewater Beach Resort
19130 Gulf Boulevard
Indian Shores, FL 33785
(813) 595-4028
(813) 595-0977 (fax)

The Edgewater Beach Resort offers unique, ground-level apartments.
All are super clean.

- $$
- 6 Units
- Cottages with fully equipped
  kitchens
- Color Cable TV
- Guest Laundry
- Grills
- Pets (no cats; dogs under 20 pounds;
  $100 deposit, $25 per stay)
- Discover
- Check-in: 2 P.M. Check-out: 10 A.M.

☞ Fairwind Cottages
19734 Gulf Boulevard
Indian Shores, FL 33785
(813) 595-4390
(800) 952-0331

Fairwind Cottages provides clean, cozy, comfortable lodgings with
private beach access and patio.

- TAC $/$$
- 15 Units
- One- and two-bedroom
  apartments with fully
  equipped kitchens
- Pool
- Color Cable TV
- Guest Laundry
- Grills
- Shuffleboard
- Pets (no pets Memorial Day through
  Labor Day)
- Fax Services
- Mastercard, VISA, Discover
- Check-in: 12 P.M. Check-out: 10 A.M.

☞ Holiday Villas III
18610 Gulf Boulevard
Indian Shores, FL 33785
(813) 595-0770
(813) 595-1932 (fax)

Holiday Villas III apartments are individually owned, completely furnished condominiums offering all the comforts of home. A private dock and fishing pier on the Intracoastal Waterway are available for guests. The Gulf-front units have balconies overlooking the beach.

- TAC $$/$$$
- 84 Units
- Condominiums; one- and two-bedroom apartments with fully equipped kitchens
- Pool
- Color Cable TV
- Guest Laundry
- Grills
- Handicapped Access
- Shuffleboard
- Fax Services
- Mastercard, VISA
- Check-in: 4 P.M. Check-out: 10 A.M.

Holiday Villas III

Island Manor Apartment Motel

19820 Gulf Boulevard
Indian Shores, FL 33785
(813) 595-2260
(813) 593-3118 (fax)
(888) 509-9833

The Island Manor features attractively furnished apartments in a beautiful, tropically landscaped setting.

- $/$$
- 11 Units
- Motel rooms; efficiencies; one- and two-bedroom apartments with fully equipped kitchens
- Pool
- Color Cable TV
- Guest Laundry
- Grills
- Handicapped Access
- Fax Services
- Mastercard, VISA
- Check-in: 2 P.M. Check-out: 10 A.M.

Island Manor Apartment Motel

☞ Paradise Palms Motel

19340 Gulf Boulevard
Indian Shores, FL 33785
(813) 595-3698
(813) 595-6347 (fax)

All rooms at Paradise Palms are located on the ground floor with Gulf views. The rooms are tastefully appointed and the kitchens include microwaves.

- $
- 7 Units
- Efficiencies with fully equipped kitchens
- Pool
- Color Cable TV
- Guest Laundry
- Grills
- Fax Services
- Mastercard, VISA
- Check-in: 2 P.M. Check-out: 10 A.M.

☞ La Regina Motel

19600 Gulf Boulevard
Indian Shores, FL 33785
(813) 595-8078
(813) 595-8078 (fax)

La Regina Motel is a two-story building that faces south. Although the rooms don't face the Gulf, they do offer a view of the water. Here you will find a family-oriented, relaxed atmosphere.

- TAC $$
- 14 Units
- One- and two-bedroom apartments with fully equipped kitchens
- Pool
- Color Cable TV
- Handicapped Access
- Pets (under 10 pounds; $25 per stay)
- Fax Services
- Mastercard, VISA, American Express
- Check-in: 2 P.M. Check-out: 10 A.M.

Fiesta Falls Adventure Golf
19463 Gulf Boulevard
Indian Shores, FL 34635
(813) 596-3784
Miniature golf and game room

Suncoast Seabird Sanctuary
18328 Gulf Boulevard
Indian Shores, FL 34635
(813) 391-6211
Largest wild bird hospital in the U.S.; home to hundreds of injured wild birds
Hours: 9 A.M. to dark
Admission: Donations gratefully accepted

Dining Out

Chateau Madrid
19519 Gulf Boulevard
Indian Shores
(813) 596-9100
Hours: 4 P.M. to 10 P.M.; Friday and Saturday until 11 P.M.
Features: authentic Spanish cuisine; casual dress; entertainment
Dinner: $10 to $19

Greenstreets
20001 Gulf Boulevard
Indian Shores
(813) 593-2077
Hours: 11:30 A.M. to 11 P.M.
Features: seafood, steak; casual waterfront dining; outside dining available; weekend entertainment
Lunch: $3.95 to $8.5
Dinner: $8.95 to $18.50

The Hungry Fisherman
19915 Gulf Boulevard
Indian Shores
(813) 595-4218
Hours: 11:30 A.M. to 10 P.M.
Features: seafood, steak, early bird specials; casual dress
Lunch: $4 to $8
Dinner: $7 to $21

The Pub
20025 Gulf Boulevard
Indian Shores
(813) 595-3172
Hours: 11 A.M. to 12 A.M.; bar open until 2 A.M.
Features: seafood, steak, sandwiches; waterside bar; piano bar nightly; casual dress
Lunch: $1.75 to $9.25
Dinner: $7 to $22

Redington Shores and Redington Beach

Accommodations

⚒ The Far Horizons Motel

17248 Gulf Boulevard
North Redington Beach, FL 33708
(813) 393-8791
(813) 391-3980 (fax)

The Far Horizons Motel offers one-bedroom efficiencies that are nicely decorated and fully equipped for your comfort and convenience.

- TAC $/$$
- 24 Units
- Efficiencies with fully equipped kitchens
- Pool
- Color Cable TV
- Guest Laundry
- Grills
- Shuffleboard
- Fax Services
- Mastercard, VISA, Discover
- Check-in: 2 P.M. Check-out: 11 A.M.

⚒ Flagship Motel

17040 Gulf Boulevard
North Redington Beach, FL 33708
(813) 391-0948
(813) 393-3488 (fax)

All rooms at the Flagship are on the ground floor. The pool is beachside.

- TAC $$
- 20 Units
- One-bedroom apartments with fully equipped kitchens
- Pool
- Hot Tub
- Color Cable TV
- Grills
- Shuffleboard
- Fax Services
- Mastercard, VISA
- Check-in: 3 P.M. Check-out: 11 A.M.

☞ The Marlin Resort Motel

17566 Gulf Boulevard
Redington Shores, FL 33708
(813) 391-0247
(813) 391-7450 (fax)
(800) 222-0493

The Marlin Motel offers tranquil surroundings with a 60-foot heated pool. If fishing is your game, the area's longest fishing pier is adjacent to the motel.

- TAC $
- 38 Units
- Motel rooms; efficiencies; one- and two-bedroom apartments with fully equipped kitchens
- Pool
- Color Cable TV

- Guest Laundry
- Grills
- Shuffleboard
- Fax Services
- Mastercard, VISA, Discover, American Express
- Check-in: 3 P.M. Check-out: 11 A.M.

☞ North Redington Beach Hilton Resort

17120 Gulf Boulevard
North Redington Beach, FL 33708
(813) 391-4000
(813) 397-0699 (fax)
(800) 447-SAND

The North Redington Beach Hilton's clean guest rooms all have private balconies overlooking the Gulf of Mexico and Boca Ciega Bay.

- TAC $$$
- 125 Units
- Hotel rooms
- Pool
- Color Cable TV
- Handicapped Access

- Restaurant/Bar
- Conference Facilities
- Fax Services
- Mastercard, VISA, Discover, American Express
- Check-in: 3 P.M. Check-out: 11 A.M.

⚭ Redington Surf Motel

17300 Gulf Boulevard
North Redington Beach, FL 33708
(813) 391-9051

At the Redington Surf, choose between a tastefully appointed and carpeted efficiency (larger than average size) and a one- or two-bedroom apartment.

- $$
- 17 Units
- Efficiencies; one- and two-bedroom apartments with fully equipped kitchens
- Pool
- Color Cable TV
- Guest Laundry
- Grills
- Shuffleboard
- Conference Facilities
- Mastercard, VISA
- Check-in: 1:30 P.M. Check-out: 10:30 A.M.

⚭ Sails Resort Motel

17004 Gulf Boulevard
North Redington Beach, FL 33708
(813) 391-6000
(813) 391-6000 (fax)

The tropically landscaped Sails Resort Motel has unusually large apartments. Some are brand new and all are tastefully furnished. Most rooms have a Gulf view. The owner lives on the premises.

- $$
- 23 Units
- Motel rooms; efficiencies; one- and two-bedroom apartments with fully equipped kitchens
- Pool
- Color Cable TV
- Guest Laundry
- Grills
- Handicapped Access
- Shuffleboard
- Fax Services
- Mastercard, VISA, Discover
- Check-in: 2 P.M. Check-out: 10 A.M.

ⓠ Sandalwood Resort

17100 Gulf Boulevard
North Redington Beach, FL 33708
(813) 397-5541
(813) 391-8098 (fax)
(800) 433-0202

The Sandalwood Beach Resort has both poolside and Gulf-front units. Rooms facing the Gulf have private balconies.

- $$
- 47 Units
- One- and two-bedroom apartments with fully equipped kitchens
- Pool
- Color Cable TV

- Guest Laundry
- Restaurant
- Conference Facilities
- Fax Services
- Mastercard, VISA, Discover, American Express
- Check-in: 2 P.M. Check-out: 10 A.M.

ⓠ Saxony Apartment Motel

16304 Gulf Boulevard
Redington Beach, FL 33708
(813) 391-9828
(813) 397-2206 (fax)
(800) 438-0677

The Gulf-front Saxony Apartment Motel has a private beach and two-bedroom cottages.

- TAC $$
- 16 Units
- Efficiencies; one- and two-bedroom apartments with fully equipped kitchens; cottages
- Pool
- Hot Tub
- Color Cable TV

- Guest Laundry
- Grills
- Handicapped Access
- Shuffleboard
- Fax Services
- Mastercard, VISA, Discover, American Express
- Check-in: 2 P.M. Check-out: 10 A.M.

✍ Sea Rocket Motel

17250 Gulf Boulevard
North Redington Beach, FL 33708
(813) 393-7485
(813) 391-1161 (fax)

The Sea Rocket Motel provides thirty individually owned and uniquely decorated one- bedroom efficiency apartments.

- $
- 30 Units
- Efficiencies with fully equipped kitchens
- Color Cable TV
- Guest Laundry

- Grills
- Shuffleboard
- Fax Services
- Mastercard, VISA
- Check-in: 2 P.M. Check-out: 11 A.M.

Sea Rocket Motel

Points of Interest

Redington Long Pier
17490 Gulf Boulevard
Redington Shores, FL 33708
(813) 391-9398
Hours: Open 24 hours
Admission: Adults, $6; children ages 11 and under, $5

Dining Out

The Lobster Pot
17814 Gulf Boulevard
Redington Shores
(813) 391-8592
Hours: 4:30 P.M. to 10:30 P.M.; Sunday, 4 P.M. to 10 P.M.
Features: seafood, steak, pasta; early bird specials; smartly casual dress
Dinner: $12.50 to $22.50

Shells
17855 Gulf Boulevard
Redington
(813) 393-8990
Hours: 12 P.M. to 10 P.M.; Friday and Saturday until 11 P.M.
Features: seafood, pasta, steak; children's menu starting at $1.95; casual dress
Lunch: $4.95 to $6.95
Dinner: $6.95 to $14.95

Wine Cellar
17307 Gulf Boulevard
Redington Beach
(813) 393-3491
Hours: 4:30 P.M. to 11 P.M.; closed Monday
Features: European atmosphere; smartly casual dress
Dinner: $10 to $30

Madeira Beach

Accommodations

The Anchorage of Madeira
14080 Gulf Boulevard
Madeira Beach, FL 33708
(813) 393-4546
(813) 393-7096 (fax)

The Anchorage offers Gulf-front rooms in a two-story building, all with private balconies.

- $
- 15 Units
- Motel rooms and efficiencies with fully equipped kitchens
- Pool
- Color Cable TV
- Guest Laundry
- Grills
- Fax Services
- Mastercard, VISA, Discover, American Express
- Check-in: 2 P.M. Check-out: 10:30 A.M.

Beach Plaza Apartment Motel
14560 Gulf Boulevard
Madeira Beach, FL 33708
(813) 391-8996
(813) 397-9689 (fax)

The Beach Plaza is a two-story building offering nicely decorated one- and two-bedroom apartments. The end units are beachfront and have balconies overlooking the Gulf.

- TAC $$
- 13 Units
- One- and two-bedroom apartments with fully equipped kitchens
- Color Cable TV
- Grills
- Handicapped Access
- Fax Services
- Mastercard, VISA, Discover, American Express
- Check-in: 3:30 P.M. Check-out: 10:30 A.M.

Crimson on the Gulf Condominium

☞ Crimson on the Gulf Condominium
12960 Gulf Boulevard
Madeira Beach, FL 33708
(813) 391-1341
(813) 393-8364 (fax)

These are large (1200–1600 square feet) one-, two- and three-bedroom luxury apartments in a modern facility. All apartments have balconies with a Gulf view and a washer and dryer for your convenience.

- TAC $$
- 15 Units
- Suites; one-, two- and three-bedroom condominiums
- Pool
- Hot Tub

- Color Cable TV
- Guest Laundry
- Handicapped Access
- Fax Services
- Mastercard, VISA, Discover
- Check-in: 3 P.M. Check-out: 10 A.M.

Holiday Inn Madeira Beach

15208 Gulf Boulevard
Madeira Beach, FL 33708
(813) 392-2275
(813) 398-1190 (fax)
(800) 360-6658

This Holiday Inn offers spacious guest rooms, a large heated pool and children's pool, tiki bar, and sports bar. A lighted tennis court is available for guests.

- TAC $$
- 149 Units
- Motel rooms
- Pool
- Color Cable TV
- Guest Laundry
- Handicapped Access
- Restaurant/Bar
- Conference Facilities
- Fax Services
- Mastercard, VISA, Discover, American Express
- Check-in: 4 P.M. Check-out: 11 A.M.

The Schooner Motel on the Gulf

14500 Gulf Boulevard
Madeira Beach, FL 33708
(813) 392-5167
(800) 573-5187

The Schooner Motel has been completely renovated. A new, heated pool overlooks the Gulf and tropical gardens.

- TAC $$
- 1 8 Units
- Motel rooms; efficiencies with microwaves; one- and two-bedroom apartments with fully equipped kitchens
- Pool
- Color Cable TV
- Guest Laundry
- Grills
- Pets (limit 2 per room; $10 and up per stay)
- Mastercard, VISA, Discover, American Express
- Check-in: 1 P.M. Check-out: 10:30 A.M.

The Schooner Motel on the Gulf

Sea Island Apartment Motel

☞ Sea Island Apartment Motel

13620 Gulf Boulevard
Madeira Beach, FL 33708
(813) 391-5893

All of the apartments at Sea Island have fully equipped kitchens with a microwave. Some of the units in this two-story building face the Gulf and have balconies or patios.

- TAC $/$$
- 15 Units
- One- and two-bedroom apartments with fully equipped kitchens
- Pool

- Color Cable TV
- Grills
- Shuffleboard
- Mastercard, VISA, Discover
- Check-in: 2:30 P.M. Check-out: 10:30 A.M.

☞ Surf Song Resort

12960 Gulf Boulevard
Madeira Beach, FL 33708
(813) 391-0284
(813) 393-8364 (fax)
(800) 237-4816

Many of the Gulf-front and Gulf-view condominiums at Surf Song have their own private balconies. All units are tastefully decorated.

- TAC $
- 40 Units
- Motel rooms; efficiencies; one- and two-bedroom condominiums with fully equipped kitchens
- Pool
- Hot Tub

- Color Cable TV
- Guest Laundry
- Grills
- Handicapped Access
- Shuffleboard
- Fax Services
- Mastercard, VISA, Discover
- Check-in: 3 P.M. Check-out: 10 A.M.

☞ Surfs Inn

14010 Gulf Boulevard
Madeira Beach, FL 33708
(813) 393-4609
(813) 391-8730 (fax)

All rooms at Surfs Inn face the beautiful beach and have nice tropical patios. Daily maid service is offered except on Sundays and holidays.

- $ / $$
- 25 Units
- Motel rooms, suites, and efficiencies with fully equipped kitchens
- Pool
- Color Cable TV

- Grills
- Shuffleboard
- Fax Services
- Mastercard, VISA, Discover, American Express
- Check-in: 2:30 P.M. Check-out: 10:30 A.M.

Points of Interest

John's Pass Village and Boardwalk (located at the south end of Madeira Beach on Gulf Boulevard)

Offers more than 100 unique shops, a variety of restaurants, boat charters, watercraft rentals, and more

Pirates Cove Adventure Golf

423 150th Avenue
Madeira Beach, FL 33708
(813) 393-8879
Miniature golf

Dining Out

Friendly Fisherman

150 128th Avenue
Madeira Beach
(813) 391-6025
Hours: 7 A.M. to 10 P.M.
Features: rustic decor with many seafood choices, good breakfast; children's menu; casual dress
Lunch: $8 to $15
Dinner: $8 to $15

Joe's Crab Shack
8790 Bay Pines Boulevard
St. Petersburg (not far from Madeira Beach)
(813) 347-2717
Hours: 11 A.M. to 10 P.M.; Friday, until 11 P.M.
Features: seafood, sandwiches; casual waterfront dining; outside dining available; children's play area (Rug Rat Zone)
Lunch: $4.99 to $6.99
Dinner: $4.99 to $14.99

Leverock's Seafood House
565 150th Avenue
Madeira Beach
(813) 393-0459
Hours: 11:30 A.M. to 10 P.M.
Features: seafood, children's menu; casual waterfront dining; free dockage
Lunch: $6 to $8
Dinner: $9 to $21

Treasure Island

Accommodations

✿ Arvilla Resort Motel

11580 Gulf Boulevard
Treasure Island, FL 33706
(813) 360-0598
(813) 363-3110 (fax)
(800) 811-5825

The Arvilla is a clean motel designed with the family in mind. It is the perfect place to get away from it all and enjoy family-oriented activities. Most of the rooms face the pool.

- $
- 14 Units
- Motel rooms; one- and two-bedroom apartments with fully equipped kitchens
- Pool
- Color Cable TV
- Guest Laundry
- Grills
- Shuffleboard
- Fax Services
- Mastercard, VISA
- Check-in: 2 P.M. Check-out: 11 A.M.

✿ Bilmar Beach Resort

10650 Gulf Boulevard
Treasure Island, FL 33706
(813) 360-5531
(813) 360-2362 (fax)
(800) 826-9724

The Bilmar Beach Resort offers nicely furnished rooms, all with two queen beds, hair dryers, safes, and refrigerators. It is conveniently located across the street from shopping and restaurants.

Arvilla Resort Motel

Bilmar Beach Resort

- TAC $$
- 172 Units
- Motel rooms and efficiencies with fully equipped kitchens
- Pool
- Hot Tub

- Color Cable TV
- Handicapped Access
- Restaurant/Bar
- Mastercard, VISA, American Express
- Check-in: 3 P.M. Check-out: 11 A.M.

✍ Captain's Quarters Inn

10035 Gulf Boulevard
Treasure Island, FL 33706
(813) 360-1659
(813) 363-3074 (fax)
(800) 526-9547

The Captain's Quarters Inn offers eight units directly on the beach. All are on the ground floor with a tropical courtyard and pool area.

- $/$$
- 9 Units
- Efficiencies and one-bedroom apartments with fully equipped kitchens
- Pool

- Color Cable TV
- Grills
- Pets (under 25 pounds; flat $20 fee)
- Mastercard, VISA
- Check-in: 2 P.M. Check-out: 10 A.M.

✍ Eldorado Motel

11360 Gulf Boulevard
Treasure Island, FL 33706
(813) 367-1991

The Eldorado is located on the Gulf and boasts the largest pool in Treasure Island. The buildings are U-shaped and all rooms face the pool.

- $
- 42 Units
- Motel rooms; one- and two-bedroom apartments with fully equipped kitchens
- Pool

- Color Cable TV
- Guest Laundry
- Grills
- Handicapped Access
- Mastercard, VISA, American Express
- Check-in: 2 P.M. Check-out: 11 A.M.

⚶ Holiday Inn

11908 Gulf Boulevard
Treasure Island, FL 33706
(813) 367-2761
(813) 367-9446 (fax)

All guest rooms at the Holiday Inn have beach views and private balconies. The hotel offers a gift shop, complimentary morning coffee and newspapers, valet laundry, and safe deposit boxes.

- TAC $$
- 110 Units
- Hotel rooms
- Pool
- Hot Tub
- Color Cable TV
- Guest Laundry
- Handicapped Access
- Restaurant/Bar
- Fax Services
- Mastercard, VISA, Discover, American Express
- Check-in: 3 P.M. Check-out: 12 P.M.

⚶ Island Inn Beach Resort

9980 Gulf Boulevard
Treasure Island, FL 33706
(813) 367-2750
(813) 360-9708 (fax)
(800) 241-9980

The Island Inn Resort offers spacious accommodations in a multistory building. Gulf-front units have balconies.

- TAC $/$$
- 101 Units
- Suites; one-, two- and three-bedroom apartments with fully equipped kitchens
- Pool
- Color Cable TV
- Guest Laundry
- Handicapped Access
- Fax Services
- Mastercard, VISA, Discover, American Express
- Check-in: 2 P.M. Check-out: 11 A.M.

⚶ Jefferson Motel Apartments

10116 Gulf Boulevard
Treasure Island, FL 33706

(813) 360-5826
(813) 367-9396 (fax)

The Jefferson Motel boasts clean, modern apartments that have a view of the Gulf from the living room.

- TAC $$
- 14 Units
- Suites
- Pool
- Color Cable TV
- Grills
- Shuffleboard
- Fax Services
- Mastercard, VISA
- Check-in: 1 P.M. Check-out: 10 A.M.

✆ Page Terrace
10500 Gulf Boulevard
Treasure Island, FL 33706
(813) 367-1997
(813) 360-7179 (fax)
(800) 532-6569

The Page Terrace has nicely appointed rooms in a three-story building. The units overlook the pool and beach, and have balconies outside the front doors.

- $/$$
- 36 Units
- Motel rooms, suites, and efficiencies with fully equipped kitchens
- Pool
- Color Cable TV
- Guest Laundry
- Grills
- Handicapped Access
- Shuffleboard
- Fax Services
- Mastercard, VISA, Discover
- Check-in: 2 P.M. Check-out: 10 A.M.

✆ The Sands of Treasure Island
11800 Gulf Boulevard
Treasure Island, FL 33706
(813) 367-1969
(813) 360-6594 (fax)

The Sands offers efficiencies and one-bedroom apartments, perfect for your family vacation. The end units have balconies overlooking the Gulf.

- TAC $
- 34 Units
- One-bedroom apartments with fully equipped kitchens
- Pool
- Color Cable TV

- Grills
- Handicapped Access
- Shuffleboard
- Fax Services
- No Credit Cards
- Check-in: 2 P.M. Check-out: 12 P.M.

〰 Sea Castle All Suite Motel
10750 Gulf Boulevard
Treasure Island, FL 33706
(813) 367-2704
(813) 360-2492 (fax)
(800) 441-8483

The Sea Castle has one-bedroom suites that sleep up to five people. Each suite is equipped with a small kitchen to help make your stay more enjoyable.

- $/$$
- 41 Units
- Suites
- Color Cable TV
- Guest Laundry
- Grills

- Handicapped Access
- Shuffleboard
- Fax Services
- Mastercard, VISA
- Check-in: 2 P.M. Check-out: 11 A.M.

Sea Castle All Suite Motel

⚑ Seahorse Cottages

10356 Gulf Boulevard
Treasure Island, FL 33706
(813) 367-2291
(813) 367-8891 (fax)
(800) 741-2291

These quaint cottages sit right in the sand! Park your car, walk across the street to the grocery store for supplies, and never leave this paradise!

- TAC $$
- 9 Units
- One- and two-bedroom apartments with fully equipped kitchens; cottages
- Color Cable TV

- Grills
- Pets (under 20 pounds; $4 per day, $25 per week)
- Fax Services
- Mastercard, VISA, Discover
- Check-in: 2 P.M. Check-out: 10 A.M.

⚑ Shifting Sands Cottages

10232 Gulf Boulevard
Treasure Island, FL 33706
(813) 360-7777
(800) 458-8728

Enjoy the Key West atmosphere of the Shifting Sands Cottages, affordably priced so you can stay longer.

- TAC $
- 8 Units
- One- and two-bedroom cottages with fully equipped kitchens
- Pool
- Color Cable TV

- Guest Laundry
- Grills
- Shuffleboard
- Mastercard, VISA, Discover, American Express
- Check-in: 2 P.M. Check-out: 10 A.M.

⚑ Suncoast Motel

10264 Gulf Boulevard
Treasure Island, FL 33706
(813) 360-9256

(813) 367-2000 (fax)
(800) 379-9428

The Suncoast Motel has a variety of accommodations. The motel has been totally renovated with new furniture and the latest appliances.

- $
- 24 Units
- Motel rooms; one- and two-bedroom apartments with fully equipped kitchens
- Pool

- Color Cable TV
- Guest Laundry
- Grills
- Shuffleboard
- Mastercard, VISA
- Check-in: 12 P.M. Check-out: 10 A.M.

☜ Surfside Motel

11270 Gulf Boulevard
Treasure Island, FL 33706
(813) 360-6551
(813) 360-4307 (fax)
http://www.surfside.com/imi/surfside

The Surfside's spacious apartments offer comfort and convenience in a relaxed beach setting.

- $$
- 10 Units
- Efficiencies; one- and two-bedroom apartments with fully equipped kitchens
- Pool
- Color Cable TV

- Guest Laundry
- Grills
- Shuffleboard
- Fax Services
- Mastercard, VISA, Discover
- Check-in: 2 P.M. Check-out: 10 A.M.

☜ Tahitian Resort

11300 Gulf Boulevard
Treasure Island, FL 33706
(813) 360-6264
(813) 367-0070 (fax)
http://www.surfside.com/imi/tahitian

The Tahitian Resort is a nice, two-story motel located within walking distance of many recreational facilities, restaurants, and shopping.

Gulf-front balconies and patios provide a nice view of the beach.

- $/$$
- 53 Units
- Motel rooms; one- and two-bedroom apartments with fully equipped kitchens
- Pool
- Color Cable TV

- Guest Laundry
- Grills
- Shuffleboard
- Fax Services
- Mastercard, VISA, Discover
- Check-in: 2 P.M. Check-out: 11 A.M.

✑ Thunderbird Beach Resort

10700 Gulf Boulevard
Treasure Island, FL 33706
(813) 367-1961
(813) 367-1961 (fax)
(800) 367-BIRD

The Thunderbird Beach Resort has spacious poolside and Gulf-front rooms and efficiencies. Gulf-front rooms feature private balconies or patios facing the beach.

- TAC $$
- 64 Units
- Motel rooms and efficiencies with fully equipped kitchens
- Pool
- Hot Tub
- Color Cable TV

- Handicapped Access
- Restaurant/Bar
- Fax Services
- Mastercard, VISA, Discover, American Express
- Check-in: 2:30 P.M. Check-out: 11 A.M.

✑ Trails End Resort Motel

11500 Gulf Boulevard
Treasure Island, FL 33706
(813) 360-5541
(813) 360-1508 (fax)

The Trails End Motel is a two-story motel with two buildings facing each other. Most units face the pool; a few offer a Gulf view.

- TAC $
- 54 Units
- Motel rooms and efficiencies with fully equipped kitchens
- Pool
- Color Cable TV
- Grills

- Handicapped Access
- Shuffleboard
- Fax Services
- Mastercard, VISA, Discover, American Express
- Check-in: 2 P.M. Check-out: 11 A.M.

Trails End Resort Motel

Points of Interest

Gulf Golf & Hoops
11605 Gulf Boulevard
Treasure Island, FL 33706
(813) 360-8143
Miniature golf and basketball hoops

Dining Out

Caddy's Waterfront
9000 West Gulf Boulevard
Sunset Beach
(813) 360-4993
Hours: 11 A.M. to 12 A.M.; Friday and Saturday, until 2 A.M.
Features: seafood, sandwiches; casual beachfront dining; entertainment
Lunch: $1.95 to $8.95
Dinner: $1.95 to $8.95

Captain Kosmakos Seafood & Steakhouse
9610 Gulf Boulevard
Treasure Island
(813) 367-3743
Hours: 3 P.M. to 2 A.M.; Sunday from 1 P.M.
Features: seafood, steak; casual dress; view of waterway and boats; children's menu
Dinner: $9 to $23

Gigi's
105 107th Avenue
Treasure Island
(813) 360-6905
Hours: 4 P.M. to 10 P.M.; Friday and Saturday until 11 P.M.
Features: Italian favorites, beer, and wine; casual dress
Dinner: $9.99 to $14.99

St. Pete Beach

Accommodations

🐚 The Alden Beach Resort

5900 Gulf Boulevard
St. Pete Beach, FL 33706
(813) 360-7081
(813) 360-5957 (fax)
(800) 237-2530

Alden Beach is a family-oriented resort offering two pools, two whirlpool spas, two tennis courts, playground, game room, and basketball court. Suites feature fully equipped kitchens and private balconies.

- $$/$$$
- 143 Units
- Motel rooms and suites
- Pool
- Hot Tub
- Color Cable TV
- Guest Laundry
- Grills
- Handicapped Access
- Shuffleboard
- Conference Facilities
- Fax Services
- Mastercard, VISA, Discover, American Express
- Check-in: 3 P.M. Check-out: 11 A.M.

🐚 Beach Haven

4980 Gulf Boulevard
St. Pete Beach, FL 33706
(813) 367-8642

Newly remodeled and beautiful, Beach Haven features one-bedroom efficiencies, motel rooms, and a heated Gulf-front pool. One unit has a Jacuzzi tub.

- TAC $
- 18 Units
- Motel rooms and efficiencies with fully equipped kitchens
- Pool
- Color Cable TV

- Guest Laundry
- Grills
- Handicapped Access
- Fax Services
- Mastercard, VISA
- Check-in: 2 P.M. Check-out: 11 A.M.

☙ Best Western Sirata Beach Resort

5390 Gulf Boulevard
St. Pete Beach, FL 33706
(813) 367-2771
(813) 360-6799 (fax)
(800) 344-5999

The Best Western Sirata offers suites and efficiencies. Suites have a king-size bed or two double beds and a pull-out queen-size sofa sleeper. Efficiencies have two double beds. The resort also features two heated pools, water sports, volleyball, children's play area, and a beach bar with weekend entertainment.

- $$$
- 155 Units
- Suites and efficiencies with fully equipped kitchens
- Pool
- Hot tub
- Color Cable TV

- Guest Laundry
- Handicapped Access
- Restaurant/Bar
- Fax Services
- Mastercard, VISA, Discover, American Express
- Check-in: 4 P.M. Check-out: 11 A.M.

☙ Bon Aire Motel

4350 Gulf Boulevard
St. Pete Beach, FL 33706
(813) 360-5596
(813) 367-6489 (fax)
(800) 360-4350

The Bon Aire Motel is a beachfront vacation paradise. This Gulf-front accommodation offers 386 feet of private beach and is a great place for the entire family.

Bon Aire Motel

- TAC $$
- 1 Units
- Motel rooms, efficiencies, and one-bedroom apartments with fully equipped kitchens
- Pool

- Color Cable TV
- Guest Laundry
- Grills
- Fax Services
- Mastercard, VISA
- Check-in: 4 P.M. Check-out: 11 A.M.

☜ Dolphin Beach Resort

4900 Gulf Boulevard
St. Pete Beach, FL 33706
(813) 360-7011
(813) 367-5909 (fax)
(800) 237-8916
http://www.dolphinbeach.com

Dolphin Beach is a large resort with a free-form pool. Conference facilities consist of 6,500 square feet of space in four rooms.

- $$
- 173 Units
- Motel rooms and efficiencies
- Pool
- Color Cable TV
- Guest Laundry
- Handicapped Access

- Restaurant/Bar
- Shuffleboard
- Conference Facilities
- Fax Services
- Mastercard, VISA, American Express
- Check-in: 4 P.M. Check-out: 11 A.M.

☞ The Don Cesar Beach Resort and Spa
3400 Gulf Boulevard
St. Pete Beach, FL 33706
(813) 360-1881
(813) 367-6952 (fax)
(800) 637-7200 (Sterling Hotels)

The Don Cesar Beach Resort and Spa is an elegant, full-service spa. This Gatsby-style resort features two pools, watersport rentals, a lavish King Charles Sunday brunch, and nearby golf, shopping, and restaurants.

- TAC $$$
- 345 Units
- Motel rooms and suites
- Pool
- Hot Tub
- Color Cable TV
- Guest Laundry
- Grills

- Handicapped Access
- Restaurant/Bar
- Fitness Center
- Conference Facilities
- Fax Services
- Mastercard, VISA, Discover, American Express
- Check-in: 4 P.M. Check-out: 12 P.M.

☞ Holiday Inn Hotel & Suites Beachfront Resort
5250 Gulf Boulevard
St. Pete Beach, FL 33706
(813) 360-1811
(813) 360-6919 (fax)
(800) 448-0901

The Holiday Inn Hotel boasts the highest revolving rooftop lounge with the most spectacular view of the beach and island. All guest rooms are completely renovated with cherry wood furniture and

The Don Cesar Beach Resort and Spa

Holdiay Inn Hotel & Suites Beachfront Resort

brass furnishings. All units have private water-view balconies, refrigerators, coffee makers, safes, and hair dryers.

- TAC $$/$$$
- 156 Units
- Hotel rooms, suites, and efficiencies with fully equipped kitchens
- Pool
- Color Cable TV
- Guest Laundry
- Handicapped Access
- Restaurant/Bar
- Fitness Center
- Conference Facilities
- Fax Services
- Mastercard, VISA, Discover, American Express
- Check-in: 4 P.M. Check-out: 11 A.M.

✑ Palm Crest Motel

3848 Gulf Boulevard
St. Pete Beach, FL 33706
(813) 360-9327

The Palm Crest Motel is a unique, Swiss Chalet–style motel on the beach.

- TAC $
- 18 Units
- Efficiencies; one- and two-bedroom apartments
- Pool
- Color Cable TV
- Guest Laundry
- Grills
- Shuffleboard
- Mastercard, VISA
- Check-in: 2 P.M. Check-out: 11 A.M.

✑ Plaza Beach Motel

4506 Gulf Boulevard
St. Pete Beach, FL 33706
(813) 367-2791
(813) 367-3620 (fax)
(800) 257-8998

The Plaza Beach Motel is newly remodeled including new furniture, carpet, tile and drapes. All rooms have microwaves.

- $$
- 39 Units
- Motel rooms and one-bedroom apartments with fully equipped kitchens
- Pool
- Color Cable TV
- Guest Laundry

- Grills
- Handicapped Access
- Shuffleboard
- Fax Services
- Mastercard, VISA, Discover, American Express
- Check-in: 3 P.M. Check-out: 11 A.M.

☞ Quality Inn Beachfront Resort

5300 Gulf Boulevard
St. Pete Beach, FL 33706
(813) 360-6911
(813) 360-6172 (fax)
(800) 370-5399

The Quality Inn Beachfront Resort offers recently renovated rooms, each with a king-size bed or two double beds, coffee makers, and safe for a small fee. There is a beach bar with weekend entertainment and a game room for all who like to play.

- $$/$$$
- 148 Units
- Hotel rooms
- Pool
- Hot Tub
- Color Cable TV
- Guest Laundry

- Handicapped Access
- Restaurant/Bar
- Conference Facilities
- Fax Services
- Mastercard, VISA, Discover, American Express
- Check-in: 4 P.M. Check-out: 11 A.M.

☞ Radisson Sandpiper Beach Resort

6000 Gulf Boulevard
St. Pete Beach, FL 33706
(813) 562-1212
(813) 562-1222 (fax)
(800) 237-0707 (Radisson and Trade Winds)

The Radisson Sandpiper is a large resort located just 30 minutes from the Tampa International Airport. Most guest rooms feature a wet bar, refrigerator, toaster, and coffee maker, while suites offer the convenience of a kitchen, living area, and private bedroom.

- TAC $$/$$$
- 159 Units
- Hotel rooms and suites
- Pool
- Color Cable TV
- Guest Laundry
- Grills
- Handicapped Access
- Restaurant/Bar
- Shuffleboard
- Fitness Center
- Conference Facilities
- Fax Services
- Mastercard, VISA, Discover
- Check-in: 4 P.M. Check-out: 12 P.M.

⚡ Sun & Sea Resort Motel
3910 Gulf Boulevard
St. Pete Beach, FL 33706
(813) 367-8273
(813) 367-8273 ext. 197 (fax)

Sun & Sea Resort Motel offers a heated pool, private beach, tropical gardens, and sun deck. Their bayside motel across the street offers a fishing and boat dock.

- $$
- 22 Units
- Motel rooms; efficiencies; one-
  and two-bedroom apartments
  with fully equipped kitchens
- Pool
- Color Cable TV
- Guest Laundry
- Grills
- Shuffleboard
- Fax Services
- Mastercard, VISA, Discover,
  American Express
- Check-in: 2 P.M. Check-out: 11 A.M.

⚡ Trade Winds Resort on St. Pete Beach
5600 Gulf Boulevard
St. Pete Beach, FL 33706
(813) 562-1212
(813) 562-1222 (fax)
(800) 237-0707 (Trade Winds and Radisson)
http://www.tradewindsresort.com

The Trade Winds is a large, convention resort with 30,000 square feet of meeting space. The resort features a tropical atmosphere with Victorian gazebos, gondolas, and waterway. The rooms are tastefully decorated and include a coffee maker, toaster, and wet bar.

- TAC $$$
- 577 Units
- Hotel rooms; one- and two-bedroom suites with fully equipped kitchens
- Pool
- Color Cable TV
- Guest Laundry
- Grills

- Handicapped Access
- Restaurant/Bar
- Shuffleboard
- Fitness Center
- Conference Facilities
- Fax Services
- Mastercard, VISA, Discover, American Express
- Check-in: 4 P.M. Check-out: 12 P.M.

Trade Winds Resort on St. Pete Beach

Points of Interest

Fort DeSoto Park
Pinellas Bayway South
Tierra Verde
(813) 866-2484
Two fishing piers, swimming beaches, picnic areas, historic fort built in 1898, camping, and boat ramp; nice paths for rollerblading and bicycling

Great Explorations
1120 4th Street South
St. Petersburg, FL 33701
(813) 821-8885
Features "hands-on" exhibits for all ages
Hours: Monday-Saturday, 10 A.M. to 5 P.M.; Sunday, 12 P.M. to 5 P.M.
Admission: Adults, $6; children ages 3 to 17, $5; children 2 and under, free

The Pier (located at the end of 2nd Avenue NE on the waterfront in downtown St. Petersburg)
(813) 821-6164
Shops and restaurants

Polynesian Putter
4999 Gulf Boulevard
St. Pete Beach, FL 33706
(813) 360-9678
Miniature golf

Salvador Dali Museum
1000 3rd Street South
St. Petersburg, FL 33701
(813) 823-3767
Home to the world's largest collection of Salvador Dali's works
Hours: Monday through Saturday, 9:30 A.M. to 5:30 P.M.; Sunday, 12 P.M. to 5:30 P.M.

Admission: Adults, $8; seniors, $7; students with ID, $4; children under 10, free

Dining Out

La Croisette
7401 Gulf Boulevard
St. Pete Beach
(813) 360-2253
Hours: 7 A.M. to 2:30 P.M.
Features: American cuisine with a French accent, great breakfast fare; casual dining
Lunch: $3.50 to $6.50

Kinjo
4615 Gulf Boulevard
St. Pete Beach
(813) 367-6762
Hours: 5 P.M. to 10 P.M.; Friday and Saturday, until 10:30 P.M.
Features: stunning Japanese restaurant, sushi bar; children's menu; early bird specials
Dinner: $5.75 to $22

Mulligan's
9524 Blind Pass Road
St. Pete Beach
(813) 367-6680
Hours: 11 A.M. to 1:30 A.M.
Features: seafood, steak, chicken; children's menu; casual waterfront dining; outside deck
Lunch: $4.25 to $12.95
Dinner: $4.25 to $12.95

Woody's Waterfront
7308 Sunset Way
St. Pete Beach
(813) 360-9165

Hours: 11 A.M. to 11 P.M.; Friday and Saturday until 12 A.M.; bar open until 1:30 A.M.

Features: sandwiches, patio food; casual waterfront dining; entertainment

Lunch: $2 to $6.75

Dinner: $2 to $6.75

SUNCOAST AREA POINTS OF INTEREST

The following attractions are all easily accessible from the beaches on the Suncoast.

Adventure Island
4545 Bougainvillea Avenue
Tampa, FL 33617
(813) 987-5600
This Anheiser-Busch water theme park features giant water slides, body flumes, wave pool, children's area, picnic and beach volleyball facilities, and lots more.
Hours: Vary depending on season; best to call. Closed from November to mid-March
Admission: Adults, $23.45; children ages 3 to 9, $21.30; children 2 and under, free
Note: Local papers and McDonald's Restaurants frequently have discount coupons to Adventure Island.

Busch Gardens
3000 East Busch Boulevard
Tampa, FL 33612
(813) 987-5082
An African theme park featuring exotic animals, amusement rides, restaurants, and shows.
Hours: Vary depending on season; best to call
Admission: Adults, $38.45; children ages 3 to 9, $32.05; children 2 and under, free

Note: Local papers and McDonald's Restaurants frequently have discount coupons to Busch Gardens.

Coral Sea Aquarium
850 Dodecanese Boulevard
Tarpon Sponge Docks
Tarpon Springs, FL 34689
(813) 938-5378
This living reef features a tidal pool, touch tank, and 100,000-gallon Caribbean reef tank and Pacific reef aquariums. Scuba divers handfeed seven- to eight-foot lemon sharks!
Hours: 10 A.M. to 5 P.M. daily
Admission: Adults, $4; seniors, $3.25; children ages 3 to 11, $2; children 2 and under, free

Florida Aquarium
701 Channelside Drive
Tampa, FL 33602
(813) 273-4020
This three-level facility depicts Florida's diverse water habitats. More than 4,300 plants and animals representing 550 species native to Florida are exhibited in a unique setting.
Hours: 9:30 A.M. to 5 P.M. daily
Admission: Adults, $13.95; children ages 3 to 12, $6.95; children 2 and under, free

Honeymoon Island State Park
One Causeway Boulevard
Dunedin, FL 34698
(813) 469-5942
This three-mile-long island, accessible by car, is located just off the Dunedin Causeway. You can sunbathe, swim, fish, and see a variety of plants and shore birds. From Honeymoon Island you can take a ferry to Caladesi Island ($4 per person round trip).
Hours: 8 A.M. to sunset
Admission: $4 per car

Lowry Park Zoological Garden
7530 North Boulevard
Tampa, FL 33604
(813) 932-0245
A zoo featuring animals in their natural habitats
Hours: 9:30 A.M. to 5 P.M. daily
Admission: Adults, $7.50; seniors, $6.50; children ages 3 to 11, $4.95; children 2 and under, free

SUNCOAST AREA GOLF

(Semi-private and Public)

Airco Golf Course
3650 Roosevelt Boulevard
Largo
(813) 573-4653
Public; driving range

Bardmoor Golf Club
8000 Bardmoor Boulevard
Largo
(813) 397-0483
Semi-private

Bay Pointe Golf Club
9399 Commodore Drive
Seminole
(813) 595-2095
Semi-private

Belleview Mido Country Club
1501 Indian Rocks Road
Belleair
(813) 581-5498
Semi-private; driving range

Chi Chi Rodriguez
3030 McMullen Booth Road
Clearwater

(813) 726-4673
Public

Clearwater Country Club
525 North Betty Lane
Clearwater
(813) 443-5078
Semi-private; driving range

Clearwater Golf Park, Inc.
1875 Airport Drive
Clearwater
(813) 447-5272
Public; driving range

Countryside Executive Golf Course
2506 Countryside Boulevard
Clearwater
(813) 796-1555
Public

East Bay Country Club
702 Country Club Drive
Largo
(813) 581-3333
Semi-private; driving range

119

Glen Oaks Golf Course
1345 Court Street
Clearwater
(813) 446-5821
Public

Largo Municipal Golf Course
12500 131st Street
Largo
(813) 587-6724
Public

Mainlands Golf Course
9445 Mainlands Boulevard
Pinellas Park
(813) 577-4847
Semi-private

Mangrove Bay Golf Course
875 62nd Avenue NE
St. Petersburg, FL
(813) 893-7797
Public; driving range

Pinecrest Golf Course
1200 Eighth Avenue SW
Largo
(813) 584-6497
Public

St. Andrews Golf Course
620 Palm Boulevard
Dunedin
(813) 733-5061
Public; driving range

CHAMBERS OF COMMERCE

Clearwater Beach Chamber of Commerce
100 Coronado Drive
Clearwater, FL 34630
(813) 447-7600

Convention and Visitors Bureau
1 Stadium Drive, Suite A
St. Petersburg, FL 33705
(813) 582-7892
(800) 345-6710

Madeira Beach Chamber of Commerce
501 150th Avenue
Madeira Beach, FL 33708
(813) 391-7373

St. Pete Beach Area Chamber of Commerce
6990 Gulf Boulevard
St. Pete Beach, FL 33706
(813) 360-6957

St. Petersburg/Clearwater Area Twin Brooks Municipal Golf Course
3800 22nd Avenue South
St. Petersburg
(813) 893-7445
Public; driving range

Treasure Island Chamber of Commerce
152 108th Avenue
Treasure Island, FL 33706
(813) 367-4529

Sarasota/Manatee Beaches

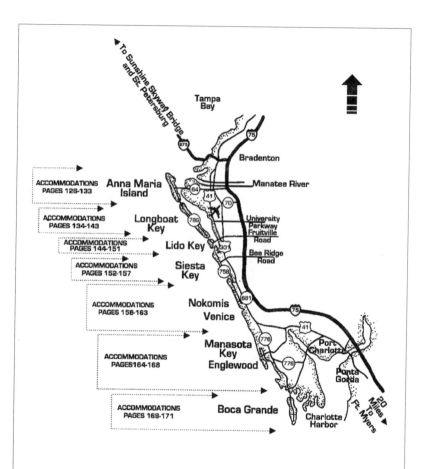

To Sunshine Skyway Bridge
and St. Petersburg

Tampa
Bay

275

75

Bradenton

ACCOMMODATIONS
PAGES 128-133

Anna Maria
Island

Manatee River

64

41

70

ACCOMMODATIONS
PAGES 134-143

Longboat
Key

789

University
Parkway
Fruitville
Road

ACCOMMODATIONS
PAGES 144-151

Lido Key

301

Bee Ridge
Road

ACCOMMODATIONS
PAGES 152-157

Siesta
Key

758

ACCOMMODATIONS
PAGES 158-163

Nokomis
Venice

681

75

ACCOMMODATIONS
PAGES 164-168

Manasota
Key
Englewood

776

41

776

Port
Charlotte

Ponta
Gorda

ACCOMMODATIONS
PAGES 169-171

Boca Grande

Charlotte
Harbor

20
Miles
To
Ft. Myers

SARASOTA/MANATEE BEACHES

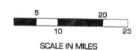

5   20

10   25

SCALE IN MILES

Overview

*T*he Sarasota/Manatee beaches are located just south of the Tampa Bay area, over the scenic Sunshine Skyway Bridge.

Anna Maria is a seven- mile barrier island with white, sandy beaches and a laid-back atmosphere. At the northern end of the island is Bayfront Park, which is on Tampa Bay and provides a spectacular view of the Sunshine Skyway Bridge. The facility offers restrooms, picnic areas, playground, and two nearby fishing piers. Anna Maria has two public beach areas, Manatee and Coquina. Manatee Public Beach, with restrooms, showers, and picnic areas, is located in Holmes Beach and is a popular spot for many visitors. Coquina Beach is located at the south end of Anna Maria Island, north of Longboat Pass, and offers a beautiful, wide beach and nice playground. Grills and picnic tables are nestled among the pine trees. A concession stand, restrooms, and shower facilities are also available.

Longboat Key, with one small public beach area and no facilities, is a nice place to go to escape the crowds. The area is famous for exclusive estates set among lush tropical foliage. Fine shops and restaurants are located along Gulf of Mexico Drive. Some of the shopping centers sit back off the road, so keep your eyes open for them.

Most of Lido Key is the public beach area. Restrooms and showers are available, and parking is free in the municipal parking lot and along Ben Franklin Drive. Lido Key is conveniently located just minutes from downtown Sarasota. An array of unique shops and restaurants are nearby on St. Armands Circle.

Siesta Key is renowned for its white, sugar-fine sandy beaches. The public beach area offers free parking, restrooms, and watercraft rentals. Crescent Beach is located two miles south of the Siesta Public Beach. The same soft sand can be found there, but this beach has no facilities. Turtle Beach, located at the south end of Siesta Key, offers a nice beach area with facilities. The sand is coarser but better for shelling.

Nokomis stretches from Casey Key to I-75. This community is mostly residential and the beaches are quite peaceful. The sands on the Venice beaches provide a beautiful spot for vacationers. Venice is famous for its fossilized sharks' teeth, which can be found in the sand as you stroll down the beach. Venice has public beach areas with ample free parking, a fishing pier, restrooms, and showers. A charming shopping area is located in downtown Venice on West Venice Avenue.

Just south of Venice is Manasota Key. This is a very quiet area with beautiful homes and a few motels. Manasota Beach is a lovely, fourteen-acre stretch of beach complete with sand dunes and sea oats. Blind Pass, also known as Middle Beach, is a scenic area, ideal for swimming and fishing. Englewood is located about two-thirds down the West coast, 85 miles south of Tampa and 50 miles north of Fort Myers. Beachcombing along Englewood Beach can be exciting as you find more prehistoric sharks' teeth buried in the sand.

Boca Grande, a village located on Gasparilla Island, is world renowned for tarpon fishing. Boca Grande Pass is one of Florida's deepest natural inlets. Every year from May through August thousands of giant tarpon, weighing in at over 150 pounds, fill the pass. There are many local marinas and captains who charter both sightseeing and fishing trips. To reach Boca Grande by car, you must travel over the toll bridge ($3.20). Specialty shops are found in downtown Boca Grande at the Railroad Depot and Railroad Plaza. There are restaurants on the island to suit every taste and budget.

Climate

(Temperature by Degrees Farenheight)

SEASON	AVERAGE LOW	AVERAGE HIGH	GULF WATER
January–March	52	77	60s–70s
April–June	64	83	70s–80s
July–September	75	91	80s
October–December	53	85	70s–80s

Getting There

By Air

Sarasota Bradenton International Airport
(941) 359-2770
Location: US Highway 41 and University Parkway

By Car

INTERSTATE 75: From I-75 traveling north or south, exit west on SR 64 (Exit 42) to get to Anna Maria and the north end of Longboat Key. Exit west on Fruitville Road (Exit 39) for Longboat Key and Lido Beach. Exit west on Bee Ridge Road (Exit 37) or Clark Road (Exit 37) for Siesta Key. Exit west on 681 (Exit 36) for Nokomis and west on Jacaranda Boulevard (Exit 35) to access Venice, Manasota Key, and Boca Grande.

US 41 (Tamiami Trail): US 41 also runs north and south and is closer to the beaches than I-75, but is a much slower route.

Anna Maria Island
(Including Holmes Beach and Bradenton)

𝓞𝓞 Aquarius Beach Resort

105 39th Street
Anna Maria, FL 34217
(941) 778-7477
(941) 778-5433 (fax)

This quaint and charming resort will have you believing you've been swept away to the tropics. Stroll through the tropical garden paths to the pool or sit on the Gulf-front sundeck. It's a nice place for the entire family.

- $/$$
- 11 Units
- Suites; one- and two-bedroom apartments with fully equipped kitchens
- Pool
- Hot Tub
- Color Cable TV
- Guest Laundry
- Grills
- Restaurant
- Shuffleboard
- Pets ($40 deposit for dogs, $7 per day; $75 deposit for cats, $7 per day)
- Conference Facilities
- Fax Services
- Mastercard, VISA, Discover, American Express
- Check-in: 2 P.M. Check-out: 11 A.M.

𝓞𝓞 Blue Water Beach Club

6306 Gulf Drive
Holmes Beach, FL 34217
(941) 778-6688
(941) 778-5765 (fax)

Blue Water Beach Club has 29 units on two floors. All units have sliding glass doors overlooking the pool and beach.

- $$
- 29 Units
- Motel rooms and one-bedroom apartments with fully equipped kitchens
- Pool
- Color Cable TV

- Grills
- Handicapped Access
- Shuffleboard
- Fax Services
- Mastercard, VISA
- Check-in: 2 P.M. Check-out: 11 A.M.

✍ The Breakers

2512 Gulf Drive North
Bradenton Beach, FL 34217
(941) 778-5588
(941) 778-0400 (fax)

The Breakers is a quaint accommodation offering beautiful sunsets from your private deck on your private beach.

- TAC $/$$
- 3 Units
- One-bedroom apartments with fully equipped kitchens
- Color Cable TV
- Grills

- Handicapped Access
- Pets (at owner's discretion)
- Fax Services
- No Credit Cards
- Check-in: 2 P.M. Check-out: 11 A.M.

The Breakers

The Coconuts Beach Resort

❧ The Coconuts Beach Resort

100 73rd Street
Holmes Beach, FL 34217
(941) 778-2277
(941) 778-2639 (fax)
(800) 331-2508

The Coconuts offers fully furnished one- and two-bedroom apartments. Some of the units face the Gulf while others open up to the pool or courtyard. Complimentary newspapers are delivered daily.

- $$
- 18 Units
- One- and two-bedroom apartments with fully equipped kitchens
- Pool
- Color Cable TV
- Guest Laundry
- Grills
- Fax Services
- Mastercard, VISA, Discover
- Check-in: 3 P.M. Check-out: 11 A.M.

∞ Econo Lodge Surfside

2502 Gulf Drive
Bradenton Beach, FL 34217
(941) 778-6671
(941) 778-0360 (fax)

All rooms at the Econo Lodge Surfside were totally renovated in 1996. Gulf-front units have balconies.

- TAC $$
- 45 Units
- Motel rooms and efficiencies with fully equipped kitchens
- Pool
- Color Cable TV
- Guest Laundry
- Grills
- Handicapped Access
- Fax Services
- Mastercard, VISA, Discover, American Express
- Check-in: 3 P.M. Check-out: 11 A.M.

∞ Harrington House Beachfront Bed & Breakfast

5626 Gulf Drive
Holmes Beach, FL 34217
(941) 778-5444
(941) 778-0527

You will embrace the casual elegance and intimate charm of Harrington House. The tropical landscaping is gorgeous. All guest rooms are uniquely decorated and have private baths and color TV. Most have French doors leading to balconies which overlook the pool and Gulf. Full breakfast is provided. Complimentary bicycles and kayaks are available for guests.

- TAC $$$
- 12 Units
- Rooms with private baths
- Pool
- Hot Tub
- Color Cable TV
- Grills
- Mastercard, VISA
- Check-in: 3 P.M. Check-out: 11 A.M.

Harrington House Beachfront Bed & Breakfast

⚙️ Sandy Toes

2518 Gulf Drive
Bradenton Beach, FL 34217
(941) 778-2333
(941) 778-0400 (fax)

Sandy Toes is quaint, quiet, and very personalized. It is a "homey" alternative to a big resort and offers a nice deck overlooking the beach.

- TAC $$
- 3 Units
- One- and two-bedroom apartments with fully equipped kitchens
- Color Cable TV
- Grills
- Handicapped Access
- Pets (deposit variable)
- No credit cards
- Check-in: 2 P.M. Check-out: 11 A.M.

Sandy Toes

🐚 **Seaside Motel**
2200 Gulf Drive North
Bradenton Beach, FL 34217
(941) 778-5254
(800) 447-7124

Seaside Motel has rooms and efficiencies in a charming, newly reno-vated, two-story building. All rooms have a beautiful view of the Gulf.

- $$$
- 10 Units
- Motel rooms and efficiencies with fully equipped kitchens
- Color Cable TV

- Grills
- Mastercard, VISA, Discover
- Check-in: 3 P.M. Check-out: 11 A.M.

131

✆ White Sands Resort

6504 Gulf Drive
Holmes Beach, FL 34217
(941) 778-2577
http://www.members.aol.com/wsresort/index.html

The White Sands Resort offers motel rooms, one- and two-bedroom apartments, and cottages, all with kitchens. It is conveniently located close to restaurants.

- $/$$
- 21 Rooms
- Motel rooms; one- and two-bedroom apartments with fully equipped kitchens; cottages

- Pool
- Color Cable TV
- Grills
- Shuffleboard
- No credit cards
- Check-in: 2 P.M. Check-out: 10 A.M.

Points of Interest

Anna Maria City Pier (located at the north end of Anna Maria Island) The pier extends into Anna Maria Sound.
Admission: Free

Rod and Reel Pier (located at the north end of Anna Maria Island) The pier extends into Anna Maria Sound.
Admission: Free for visitors; nominal fee for anglers

Dining Out

Beach Bistro
6600 Gulf Drive
Holmes Beach
(941) 778-6444
Hours: 5:30 P.M. to 10 P.M.
Features: seafood, steak, great desserts; elegant beachfront dining
Dinner: $18 to $27

Beach House
200 Gulf Drive
Bradenton Beach
(941) 779-2222
Hours: 11:30 A.M. to 10:30 P.M.
Features: seafood, sandwiches; casual beachfront dining; entertainment nightly
Lunch: $4.95 to $12.95
Dinner: $5.95 to $18.95

Rotten Ralph's
902 South Bay Boulevard (in the Anna Maria Yacht Basin)
Anna Maria
(941) 778-3953
Hours: 11 A.M. to 10 P.M.
Features: seafood, sandwiches, famous for fish-and-chips; casual waterfront dining
Lunch: $5.25 to $6.95
Dinner: $9.95 to $16.95

Sandbar Restaurant
100 Spring Street
Anna Maria
(941) 778-0444
Hours: 11:30 A.M. to 10 P.M.
Features: seafood, sandwiches, early bird specials; casual beachfront dining; entertainment nightly
Lunch: $5.95 to $9.95
Dinner: $11.95 to $16.95 (inside), $9.95 to $17.95 (deck)

Longboat Key

Accommodations

☞ Cabana Beach Club

5851 Gulf of Mexico Drive
Longboat Key, FL 34228
(941) 383-9505
(941) 383-1830 (fax)
(800) 237-9505
http://www.longboatkey.com

The Cabana Beach Club is a wonderful, island-style resort with lush, tropically landscaped areas. Each room is beautifully decorated and fully equipped for your every vacation need.

- $$
- 10 Units
- Efficiencies; one-, two- and three-bedroom apartments with fully equipped kitchens
- Pool

- Color TV
- Guest Laundry
- Grills
- Fax Services
- Mastercard, VISA
- Check-in: 3 P.M. Check-out: 11 A.M.

☞ Cooks Holiday Lodge Resort

4235 Gulf of Mexico Drive
Longboat Key, FL 34228
(941) 383-3788
(941) 387-7966 (fax)

The Holiday Lodge is a five-story building offering spacious one-bedroom apartments with balconies over looking the Gulf in a friendly atmosphere.

- $$
- 29 Units
- One-bedroom apartments with fully equipped kitchens; cottages
- Pool
- Hot Tub
- Color Cable TV

- Guest Laundry
- Grills
- Handicapped Access
- Shuffleboard
- Fax Services
- Mastercard, VISA, Discover, American Express
- Check-in: 3 P.M. Check-out: 11 A.M.

⚘ Diplomat Resort

3155 Gulf of Mexico Drive
Longboat Key, FL 34228
(941) 383-3791
(941) 383-0983 (fax)
(800) 344-5418

The Diplomat Resort has privately owned units that face the Gulf. It is an exclusive spot on Longboat Key.

- TAC $$
- 50 Units
- One- and two-bedroom apartments with fully equipped kitchens
- Pool

- Color Cable TV
- Guest Laundry
- Fax Services
- Mastercard, VISA, Discover
- Check-in: 3 P.M. Check-out: 11 A.M.

⚘ Holiday Beach Resort

4765 Gulf of Mexico Drive
Longboat Key, FL 34228
(941) 383-3704
(941) 383-0546 (fax)

The Holiday Beach Resort has beautiful accommodations. The spacious units have cathedral ceilings. A tennis court is available for guests.

- TAC $$$
- 26 Units
- One- and two-bedroom apartments with fully equipped kitchens
- Pool
- Color Cable TV
- Guest Laundry
- Grills
- Handicapped Access
- Shuffleboard
- Fax Services
- Mastercard, VISA
- Check-in: 3 P.M. Check-out: 11 A.M.

Holiday Beach Resort

🌀 Holiday Inn/Holidome Longboat Key
4949 Gulf of Mexico Drive
Longboat Key, FL 34228
(941) 383-3771
(941) 383-7871 (fax)
(800) 465-4436

This Holiday Inn is a tropical island resort with a private beach, four tennis courts, indoor and outdoor pools, a concierge desk, meeting rooms, and weekend entertainment.

- TAC $$$
- 146 Units
- Hotel rooms and suites
- Pool
- Hot Tub
- Color Cable TV
- Guest Laundry
- Handicapped Access

- Restaurant/Bar
- Shuffleboard
- Conference Facilities
- Fax Services
- Mastercard, VISA, Discover, American Express
- Check-in: 3:30 P.M. Check-out: 11 A.M.

⊘ Longboat Key Hilton Beach Resort

4711 Gulf of Mexico Drive
Longboat Key, FL 34228
(941) 383-2451
(941) 383-7979 (fax)
(800) 282-3046

The Longboat Key Hilton is an intimate, full-service resort on a private beachfront. Tennis is available for guests.

- TAC $$$
- 10 Units
- Motel rooms and suites
- Pool
- Color Cable TV
- Restaurant/Bar

- Shuffleboard
- Conference Facilities
- Fax Services
- Mastercard, VISA, Discover, American Express
- Check-in: 3 P.M. Check-out: 11 A.M.

⊘ Outrigger Resort

5155 Gulf of Mexico Drive
Longboat Key, FL 34228
(941) 383-3187

The Outrigger Resort offers beautiful accommodations with weekly maid service, ample parking, and great views.

- TAC $$
- 10 Units
- One- and two-bedroom condominiums with fully equipped kitchens

- Color Cable TV
- Guest Laundry
- Grills
- Mastercard, VISA
- Check-in: 3 P.M. Check-out: 10 A.M.

⌘ Riviera Beach Motel

5451 Gulf of Mexico Drive
Longboat Key, FL 34228
(941) 383-2552
(941) 383-2245 (fax)
http://www.sarasota-online.com/riviera/

The Riviera Beach Resort is a small, intimate resort with a secluded, tropical beach setting. The spacious units overlook tropical gardens and the calm, blue-green waters of the Gulf.

- $$
- 11 Units
- One- and two-bedroom apartments with fully equipped kitchens
- Color Cable TV
- Guest Laundry
- Grills

- Handicapped Access
- Shuffleboard
- Pets (under 15 pounds; $50 deposit, $10 per night)
- Fax Services
- Mastercard, VISA, Discover, American Express
- Check-in: 2 P.M. Check-out: 10 A.M.

⌘ Sea Bird Beach Resort

3465 Gulf of Mexico Drive
Longboat Key, FL 34228
(941) 383-1636
(941) 383-4419 (fax)

The Sea Bird Beach Resort is a friendly motel with lots of charm. All rooms are spotless and have a breathtaking view of the Gulf.

- $$
- 14 Units
- Efficiencies; one- and two-bedroom apartments with fully equipped kitchens
- Pool
- Color Cable TV

- Guest Laundry
- Grills
- Fax Services
- Mastercard, VISA, Discover, American Express
- Check-in: 3 P.M. Check-out: 11 A.M.

Sea Bird Beach Resort

Sea Club I
4141 Gulf of Mexico Drive
Longboat Key, FL 34228
(941) 383-2431

The Sea Club I is conveniently located near shopping and dining yet located off the beaten path for a carefree getaway.

- $$
- 24 Units
- One- and two-bedroom apartments with fully equipped kitchens
- Pool
- Color Cable TV
- Guest Laundry
- Grills
- Handicapped Access
- Fax Services
- Mastercard, VISA
- Check-in: 2 P.M. Check-out: 10 A.M.

Sea Club I

℘ Sea Horse Beach Resort

3453 Gulf of Mexico Drive
Longboat Key, FL 34228
(941) 383-2417
(941) 387-8771 (fax)

The Seahorse Beach Resort has beautiful apartments that overlook the sparkling Gulf waters, providing an ever-changing vista from the soft light of early morning to the last rays of sunset.

- $$$
- 35 Units
- One- and two-bedroom apartments with fully equipped kitchens
- Pool
- Color Cable TV
- Guest Laundry
- Grills
- Fax Services
- Mastercard, VISA, Discover
- Check-in: 3 P.M. Check-out: 11 A.M.

Sea Horse Beach Resort

🌀 **Silver Sands**
5841 Gulf of Mexico Drive
Longboat Key, FL 34228
(941) 383-3731
(941) 778-4308 (fax)
(800) 245-3731

Newly renovated, all the units at the Silver Sands have refrigerators and most have a Gulf view. A tennis court is available for guest use.

- TAC $$/$$$
- 36 Units
- One- and two-bedroom apartments with fully equipped kitchens
- Pool
- Color Cable TV
- Guest Laundry
- Grills
- Shuffleboard
- Fax Services
- Mastercard, VISA, Discover, American Express
- Check-in: 2 P.M. Check-out: 11 A.M.

☞ Starfish Motel
2929 Gulf of Mexico Drive
Longboat Key, FL 34228
(941) 383-1511

The Starfish has an old, rustic look. The rooms are comfortable and cozy. You'll feel right at home in the cottagelike atmosphere. Five out of the six rooms directly face the Gulf.

- $$
- 6 Units
- One- and two-bedroom apartments with fully equipped kitchens
- Color Cable TV
- Guest Laundry
- Grills
- Mastercard, VISA
- Check-in: 3 P.M. Check-out: 11 A.M.

☞ Sun 'n Sea Cottages and Apartments
4651 Gulf of Mexico Drive
Longboat Key, FL 34228
(941) 383-5588
(941) 383-5588 (fax)

Sun 'n Sea offers one- and two-bedroom cottages with carports and screened porches, under a canopy of Australian pines. In addition to the cottages, you'll find efficiencies and one-bedroom deluxe suite apartments.

- $$
- 24 Units
- Efficiencies with fully equipped kitchens; one- and two-bedroom cottages
- Color Cable TV
- Guest Laundry
- Grills
- Shuffleboard
- Fax Services
- No Credit Cards
- Check-in: 3 P.M. Check-out: 10 A.M.

Points of Interest

Avenue of the Flowers
Located within the 2000 block of Gulf of Mexico Drive. Offers a variety of fine shops and restaurants

The Centre Shops
5350-5390 Gulf Boulevard
In addition to fine shops and restaurants, you will also find several art galleries.

Dining Out

Buccaneer Inn Marina
595 Dream Island Road
Longboat Key
(941) 383-5565
Hours: 12 P.M. to 9:30 P.M.; Friday and Saturday until 10 P.M.; lounge open until 11 P.M.
Features: seafood, prime rib, children's menu, early bird specials; casual waterfront dining
Lunch: $3.95 to $11.95
Dinner: $7.95 to $18.95

Euphemia Haye
5540 Gulf of Mexico Drive
Longboat Key
(941) 383-3633
Hours: 5:30 P.M. to 10:30 P.M.; lounge and dessert room, 6 P.M. to 12 A.M.
Features: eclectic menu, seafood specials; entertainment; smartly casual dress
Dinner: $18 to $34

Lynches Landing
4000 Gulf of Mexico Drive
Longboat Key
(941) 383-0791
Hours: 11:30 A.M. to 12 A.M.; Sunday from 3:30 P.M.
Features: fresh fish daily, Irish specialties, children's menu, early bird specials; casual dress
Lunch: $4 to $9
Dinner: $5 to $21

Lido Key

Accommodations

℘ Azure Tides Resort

1330 Ben Franklin Drive
Sarasota, FL 34236
(941) 388-2101
(941) 388-3015 (fax)
(800) 326-8433

The Azure Tides Resort features 33 Gulf-view hotel rooms and 32 one- and two-bedroom apartments with separate living and dining areas and complete kitchens.

- TAC $$$
- 65 Units
- Hotel rooms; one- and two-bedroom apartments with fully equipped kitchens
- Pool
- Color Cable TV
- Guest Laundry
- Handicapped Access
- Pets (under 20 pounds; $50 deposit)
- Conference Facilities
- Fax Services
- Mastercard, VISA, Discover, American Express
- Check-in: 3 P.M. Check-out: 11 A.M.

℘ Coquina on the Beach

1008 Ben Franklin Drive
Sarasota, FL 34236
(941) 388-2141
(941) 388-3017 (fax)
(800) 833-2141

Coquina on the Beach has efficiencies and one- and two-bedroom apartments, all with fully equipped kitchens. Some rooms face the tropically landscaped pool area while others overlook the beach. St. Armands Circle is within walking distance.

Coquina on the Beach

- TAC $$$
- 34 Units
- Efficiencies; one- and two-bed-room apartments with fully equipped kitchens
- Pool
- Color Cable TV
- Guest Laundry
- Grills
- Shuffleboard
- Pets ($25 per stay for one pet, $35 for two or more pets)
- Fax Services
- Mastercard, VISA, Discover, American Express
- Check-in: 3 P.M. Check-out: 11 A.M.

✇ Gulf Beach Motel
930 Ben Franklin Drive
Sarasota, FL 34236
(941) 388-2127
(941) 388-1312 (fax)
(800) 232-2489

The Gulf Beach Motel offers a private sandy beach in a quiet area. A typical motel with rooms facing the parking lot, it is just a short distance from restaurants and shops.

- $$
- 49 Units
- Motel rooms; efficiencies; one- and two-bedroom apartments with fully equipped kitchens
- Pool
- Color Cable TV

- Guest Laundry
- Grills
- Shuffleboard
- Fax Services
- Mastercard, VISA
- Check-in: 3 P.M. Check-out: 11 A.M.

෴ Half Moon Beach Club

2050 Ben Franklin Drive
Sarasota, FL 34236
(941) 388-3694
(941) 388-1938 (fax)
(800) 358-3245
http://www.halfmoon-lidokey.com

The Half Moon Beach Club offers a wide selection of beautifully furnished suites, efficiencies and rooms to fit every budget and need. All rooms have a patio or balcony, refrigerator, and coffee maker. Some rooms have kitchenettes equipped with microwaves.

- TAC $$$
- 85 Units
- Motel rooms, suites, and efficiencies with fully equipped kitchens
- Pool
- Color Cable TV
- Guest Laundry

- Handicapped Access
- Restaurant/Bar
- Conference Facilities
- Fax Services
- Mastercard, VISA, Discover, American Express
- Check-in: 3 P.M. Check-out: 11 A.M.

෴ Harley Sandcastle Hotel

1540 Ben Franklin Drive
Sarasota, FL 34236
(941) 388-2181
(941) 388-2655 (fax)
(800) 321-2323

Located on 600 feet of private sandy beach, the Harley is a large resort offering a candelight restaurant, sidewalk cafe, lounge, pool bar, two

Half Moon Beach Club

Harley Sandcastle Hotel

pools, gift shop, and water sports including sailboats, kayaks, and windsurfers.

- TAC $$/$$$
- 179 Units
- Hotel rooms
- Pool
- Color Cable TV
- Guest Laundry
- Handicapped Access

- Restaurant/Bar
- Shuffleboard
- Conference Facilities
- Fax Services
- Mastercard, VISA, Discover, American Express
- Check-in: 3 P.M. Check-out: 11 A.M.

Radisson Lido Beach Resort
700 Ben Franklin Drive
Sarasota, FL 34236
(941) 388-2161
(941) 388-3175 (fax)
(800) 333-3333

This completely renovated 116-unit Radisson offers beach recreation (sail boats, jet ski, fishing, snorkeling, etc.), refrigerators, microwaves, and coffee makers. Almost all of the rooms have a Gulf view.

- TAC $$/$$$
- 116 Units
- Suites and efficiencies with fully equipped kitchens
- Pool
- Color Cable TV
- GuestLaundry
- Grills

- Handicapped Access
- Restaurant/Bar
- Conference Facilities
- Fax Services
- Mastercard, VISA, Discover, American Express
- Check-in: 4 P.M. Check-out: 12 P.M.

Points of Interest

The John and Mable Ringling Museum of Art
5401 Bay Shore Road
Sarasota
(941) 359-5700

This museum houses one of the world's most important collections of Baroque paintings. For one admission price you can enjoy the art museum, the Circus Museum, and Cà d'Zan (the Ringling residence).

Radisson Lido Beach Resort

Hours: 10 A.M. to 5:30 P.M., daily
Admission: Adults, $8.50; seniors, $7.50; children ages 12 and under, free with an adult; teachers and students, free with identification

Marie Selby Botanical Gardens
711 Palm Avenue
Sarasota
(941) 366-5731 ext.10
Features beautiful gardens, grounds, and boardwalk.
Hours: 10 A.M. to 5 P.M., daily
Admission: Adults, $7; children ages 6 to 11, $3; children under 6, free

Mote Marine Aquarium
1600 Ken Thompson Parkway
Sarasota
(941) 388-4441
An educational research center featuring Florida marine life dis-

played in over thirty-five aquariums
Hours: 10 A.M. to 5 P.M., daily
Admission: Adults, $8; children ages 4 to 18, $6; children under 4, free

Pelican Man's Bird Sanctuary
1708 Ken Thompson Parkway
Sarasota
(941) 388-4444
Sanctuary dedicated to the rescue and rehabilitation of pelicans and other wild birds
Hours: 10 A.M. to 5 P.M. daily
Admission: Donations gladly accepted

Sarasota Jungle Gardens
3701 Bay Shore Road
Sarasota
(941) 355-5305
A tropical paradise featuring wild animals, exotic birds, and a spectacular butterfly collection
Hours: 9 A.M. to 5 P.M., daily
Admission: Adults, $9; Seniors, $7; children ages 3 to 12, $5; children under 3, free

South Lido Park (located at the south end of Lido Key)
This is a Sarasota County Park offering volleyball, playground, grills, picnic tables, beach area, and restrooms. Animals are not allowed in the park.
St. Armands Circle (located on St. Armands Key)
Sarasota
A world-renowned center of exclusive retailers and restaurants

---

Dining Out

Columbia Restaurant
411 St. Armands Circle
Sarasota
(941) 388-3987

Hours: 11 A.M. to 11 P.M.
Features: Cuban/American cuisine, Sunday brunch, children's menu, early bird specials; smartly casual dining
Lunch: $4 to $8
Dinner: $20 to $26

Hemmingway's
325 John Ringling Boulevard
Sarasota
(941) 388-3948
Hours: 11:30 A.M. to 10 P.M.; Friday and Saturday until 11 P.M.
Features: full menu including sandwiches, children's menu; casual dress
Lunch: $3.95 to $8.95
Dinner: $8.95 to $16.95

Miramar at the Quay
216 Sarasota Quay
Sarasota
(941) 954-3332
Hours: 11:30 A.M. to 10 P.M.; Friday and Saturday until 11 P.M.; Sunday, 12 P.M. to 10 P.M.
Features: Spanish and Cuban-American cuisine, children's menu, early bird specials; casual dress; overlooking marina
Lunch: $10 to $13
Dinner: $11 to $20

Siesta Key

Accommodations

✍ Crescent View Beach Club

6512 Midnight Pass Road
Sarasota, FL 34242
(941) 349-2000
(941) 349-9748 (fax)
(800) 344-7171

The Crescent View Beach Club is located on beautiful Crescent Beach and is within walking distance of many shops and restaurants. Each condominium has its own balcony with a Gulf view.

- TAC $$$
- 26 Units
- Condominiums
- Pool
- Hot Tub
- Color Cable TV
- Guest Laundry
- Grills
- Handicapped Access
- Fax Services
- Mastercard, VISA, Discover, American Express
- Check-in: 3 P.M. Check-out: 11 A.M.

✍ Sea Club V Beach Resort

6744 Sarasea Circle
Sarasota, FL 34242
(941) 349-1176
(941) 349-7698 (fax)
(800) 475-1176

The calm, blue waters of the Gulf of Mexico and the world's "whitest, finest sand" is your private playground at the Sea Club V Beach Resort. Complimentary sailboats and beach equipment are available. Weekly rentals are preferred.

Crescent View Beach Club

- TAC $$$
- 41 Units
- One- and two-bedroom apart-
  ments with fully equipped
  kitchens
- Pool
- Hot Tub

- Color Cable TV
- Guest Laundry
- Grills
- Shuffleboard
- Fax Services
- Mastercard, VISA
- Check-in: 4 P.M. Check-out: 10 A.M.

⚘ Siesta Royale Apartments

6334 Midnight Pass Road
Sarasota, FL 34242
(941) 349-4014
(941) 349-4014 (fax)

The Siesta Royale is a nice, clean accommodation requesting a five-night minimum stay.

- $$
- 58 Units
- One- and two-bedroom
  apartments with fully
  equipped kitchens
- Pool

- Color Cable TV
- Guest Laundry
- Shuffleboard
- Fax Services
- No credit cards
- Check-in: 1 P.M. Check-out: 10 A.M.

Siesta Royale Apartments

✍ Siesta Sands

118 Beach Road
Sarasota, FL 34242
(941) 349-1929

All condominiums at Siesta Sands are equipped to sleep four people comfortably and have direct access to a Gulf-side deck. Umbrella tables and chairs are available for guests. Step onto the beach from the deck!

- TAC $$
- 16 Units
- One-bedroom condominiums with fully equipped kitchens
- Color Cable TV
- Guest Laundry
- Grills
- No Credit Cards
- Check-in: 4 P.M. Check-out: 10 A.M.

🌀 Siesta Sun Apartments

6424 Midnight Pass Road
Sarasota, FL 34242
(941) 349-8233

The Siesta Sun has comfortable, clean, affordable one- and two-bedroom apartments.

- $
- 25 Units
- One- and two-bedroom apartments with fully equipped kitchens
- Pool
- Color Cable TV
- Guest Laundry
- Grills
- Handicapped Access
- Shuffleboard
- Pets (under 20 pounds; $20 per stay)
- Fax Services
- No Credit Cards
- Check-in: 2 P.M. Check-out: 10 A.M.

🌀 Surfrider Motel & Beach Apartments

6400 Midnight Pass Road
Sarasota, FL 34242
(941) 349-2121

The Surfrider offers you a choice of motel rooms or completely private one- and two- bedroom apartments and villas. The motel rooms overlook the beach while the villas and apartments face the pool and courtyard. Most units have screened porches.

- $$
- 21 Units
- Motel rooms; one- and two-bedroom apartments with fully equipped kitchens; cottages
- Pool
- Hot Tub
- Color Cable TV
- Pets (no restrictions or fees)
- No Credit Cards
- Check-in: 2 P.M. Check-out: 11 A.M.

Surfrider Motel & Beach Apartments

Points of Interest

Myakka River State Park
(located eleven miles east of Interstate 75 on Route 72)
Sarasota
(941) 361-6515
Florida's largest state park featuring more than thirty-seven miles of nature trails, fishing, canoeing, air boat rides, and picnicking. It's a great place to spy alligators in a natural setting.
Hours: 8 A.M. to sunset daily
Admission: $4 per car (up to eight people)

Siesta Key Village
Ocean Boulevard
Over 100 unique shops and restaurants located along Ocean Boulevard

Dining Out

Coasters
1500 Stickney Point Road
Sarasota
(941) 923-4848
Hours: 11:30 A.M. to 10 P.M.; Friday and Saturday until 11 P.M.
Features: extensive menu, children's menu; casual waterfront and patio dining
Lunch: $9 to $11
Dinner: $14 to $18

Phillipi Creek Village
5353 South Tamiami Trail
Sarasota
(941) 925-4444
Hours: 11 A.M. to 10:30 P.M.; Friday until 11 P.M.
Features: oyster bar, seafood, sandwiches, popular for grouper sandwiches and shrimp; casual waterfront dining
Lunch: $3.50 to $6.95
Dinner: $3.30 to $21.95

The Summerhouse Restaurant
6101 Midnight Pass
Siesta Key
(941) 349-1100
Hours: 5 P.M. to 11 P.M.; Sunday, 11 A.M. to 3 P.M., 5 P.M. to 10 P.M.
Features: American/Continental cuisine, children's menu, Sunday brunch, early bird specials; smartly casual dress; outdoor deck dining
Dinner: $13 to $28

Nokomis/Venice

Accommodations

A Beach Retreat on Casey Key
105 Casey Key Road
Nokomis, FL 34275
(941) 485-8771
(941) 966-3758 (fax)
(888) 235-6161
http://www.venice-fla.com/beachretreat.htm

A Beach Retreat offers guests newly remodeled, spacious accommodations. It is situated on the Gulf as well as the Bay. Docks are available on the bay side.

- $$
- 20 Units
- Motel rooms; one- and two-bedroom apartments with fully equipped kitchens
- Pool
- Color Cable TV
- Guest Laundry
- Grills
- Shuffleboard
- Fax Services
- Mastercard, VISA
- Check-in: 3 P.M. Check-out: 11 A.M.

Best Western Sandbar Beach Resort
811 the Esplanade
Venice, FL 34293
(941) 488-2251
(941) 485-2894 (fax)
(800) 822-4853

The Best Western Sandbar offers beautiful accommodations in a well-maintained, four- story building.

- TAC $$$
- 44 Units
- Motel rooms and efficiencies with fully equipped kitchens
- Pool
- Color Cable TV
- Guest Laundry
- Restaurant/Bar
- Shuffleboard
- Fax Services
- Mastercard, VISA, Discover, American Express
- Check-in: 2 P.M. Check-out: 11 A.M.

Best Western Sandbar Beach Resort

🐾 Gulf Sands Beach Apartments
433 Casey Key Road
Nokomis, FL 34275
(941) 488-7272
(941) 484-6827 (fax)

Gulf Sands Beach offers comfortable accommodations close to shopping and restaurants. Small pets are welcome with a $5 per night charge.

- TAC $$$
- 11 Units
- Motel rooms; one- and two-bedroom apartments with fully equipped kitchens
- Hot Tub
- Color Cable TV
- Guest Laundry

- Grills
- Handicapped Access
- Shuffleboard
- Pets (small pets welcome; $5 per night)
- Fax Services
- Mastercard, VISA, Discover, American Express
- Check-in: 1 P.M. Check-out: 10:30 A.M.

⚭ Gulf Shore Beach Resort Motel

317 Casey Key Road
Nokomis, FL 34275
(941) 488-6210
(941) 488-9455 (fax)

Gulf Shore has apartments on both the Gulf side and the Bay side. The buildings resemble villas and center around a grassy courtyard. Boat docks are available at no charge.

- $$/$$$
- 25 Units
- One- and two-bedroom apartments with fully equipped kitchens
- Color Cable TV
- Guest Laundry
- Grills

- Shuffleboard
- Pets (pets welcome except from December 20 through mid-April; $5 per night)
- Fax Services
- Mastercard, VISA, Discover, American Express
- Check-in: 12 P.M. Check-out: 10 A.M.

⚭ Gulf Surf Resort Motel

3905 Casey Key Road
Nokomis, FL 34275
(941) 966-2669

Gulf Surf has one- and two-bedroom apartments and is located in a private, residential setting.

- $$
- 9 Units
- Motel rooms; one- and two-bedroom apartments with fully equipped kitchens

- Hot Tub
- Color Cable TV
- Guest Laundry
- Grills
- Handicapped Access

- Pets ($6 per stay)
- Mastercard, VISA
- Check-in: 3 P.M. Check-out: 11 A.M.

⟳ Island House Apartment Motel, Inc.
205 Casey Key Road
Nokomis, FL 34275
(941) 488-1719

At the Island House, every apartment opens directly onto the beach and has either a balcony or a porch.

- $$
- 14 Units
- Motel rooms and one-bedroom apartments with fully equipped kitchens

- Color Cable TV
- Grills
- Mastercard, VISA
- Check-in: 2 P.M. Check-out: 10 A.M.

Island House Apartment Motel. Inc.

⟳ Venice Villas (Heritage Realty)
908 Villas Drive
Venice, FL 34285

(941) 488-2802
(941) 488-0282 (fax)
(800) 224-8455

The Venice Villas is a great place for families. Only a few units face the Gulf; the others open up on private courtyards, the pool, or the parking lot. Weekly and monthly rates are available.

- $$
- 55 Units
- Motel rooms; one- and two-bedroom apartments with fully equipped kitchens
- Pool
- Color Cable TV
- Guest Laundry
- Grills
- Handicapped Access
- Shuffleboard
- Fax Services
- Mastercard, VISA
- Check-in: 3 P.M. Check-out: 11 A.M.

☜ Wishing Well Beach to Bay

211 Casey Key Road
Nokomis, FL 34275
(941) 488-5011

The Wishing Well is a small, clean, friendly motel located in a quiet area, yet it's still close to urban amenities.

- TAC $$
- 14 Units
- Motel rooms and one-bedroom apartments with fully equipped kitchens
- Color TV
- Grills
- Mastercard, VISA
- Check-in: 12 P.M. Check-out: 10 A.M.

Points of Interest

Oscar Scherer State Recreation Area
(located six miles north of Venice on US 41)
(941) 483-5956
The park—462 acres of pine and scrub flatwoods—features streams for canoeing, a swimming lake, nature trails, campgrounds, and picnic areas.

Hours: 8 A.M. to sunset
Admission: $3.25 per car (up to eight people)

Dining Out

The Crow's Nest
1968 Tarpon Center Drive
Venice
(941) 484-9551
Hours: 11:30 A.M. to 3 P.M., 5 P.M. to 10 P.M.; Sunday, 12 P.M. to 10 P.M.
Features: raw bar, seafood, children's menu, early bird specials; casual dress
Lunch: $7 to $11
Dinner: $13 to $21

Sharky's on the Pier
1600 South Harbor Drive
Venice
(941) 488-1456
Hours: 11:30 A.M. to 9:30 P.M.; Friday and Saturday until 10 P.M.; tiki deck Friday and Saturday until 12 A.M.
Features: fresh seafood, children's menu; casual beachfront dining
Lunch: $6 to $8
Dinner: $9 to $20

Snook Haven
5000 East Venice Avenue
Venice
(941) 484-2553
Hours: 11 A.M. to 9 P.M.; closed Tuesday
Features: seafood, steak, sandwiches; entertainment nightly; casual dining on the Myakka River; canoe rentals (open at 8 A.M.); country band and barbecue every Sunday
Lunch: $2.50 to $11.95
Dinner: $5.95 to $12.95

Manasota Key/Englewood

Accommodations

✍ Island House

2580 North Beach Road
Manasota Key, FL 33028
(954) 742-4400
(954) 742-4403 (fax)

The Island House offers breathtaking views of the Gulf. All apartments are newly decorated, private, quiet, and safe.

- TAC $$
- 5 Units
- One- and two-bedroom apartments with fully equipped kitchens
- Color Cable TV
- Grills
- Fax Services
- Check-in time: 2 P.M. Check-out: 11 A.M.

✍ Penthouse Beach Apartments

1155 Shoreview Drive
Englewood, FL 34223
(941) 474-2121

The Penthouse offers one- and two-bedroom apartments on south Manasota Key. They are clean and quiet with tropically landscaped grounds. Bikes are provided for guests. Good restaurants are nearby and shopping is just over the bridge.

- $$
- 5 Units
- One- and two-bedroom apartments with fully equipped kitchens
- Color Cable TV
- Guest Laundry
- No credit cards
- Check-in: 2 P.M. Check-out: 10 A.M.

⚘ Seaside Beach Resort
5050 North Beach Road
Englewood, FL 34223
(941) 473-3311

The Seaside Beach Resort has one- and two-bedroom apartments set in a private tropical setting with direct access to beautiful Lemon Bay and the uncrowded beaches along the Gulf of Mexico.

- $$/$$$
- 18 Units
- One- and two-bedroom apartments
- Pool
- Color Cable TV
- Guest Laundry
- Grills
- Mastercard, VISA, Discover
- Check-in: 2 P.M. Check-out: 10 A.M.

⚘ Surf and Sand
1155 Shoreline Drive #1
Englewood, FL 34223
(941) 474-2121 (Penthouse Beach Apartments)

The Surf and Sand offers well-equipped one-bedroom apartments—just bring your toothbrush and move in. The facility offers a beautiful view of the Gulf, great shelling and shark tooth collecting, and parking for boats and trailers.

- $$
- 4 Units
- One-bedroom apartments with fully equipped kitchens
- Color Cable TV
- Pets (at owner's discretion; small deposit required)
- No Credit Cards
- Check-in: 2 P.M. Check-out: 10 A.M.

⚘ Weston's Resort
985 Gulf Boulevard
Englewood, FL 34223
(941) 474-3431 ext. 0
(941) 473-4910 (fax)

Weston's Resort

Accommodations at Weston's Resort range from studio efficiencies to three-bedroom units along 900 feet of Gulf beach and 500 feet of Bayfront. Amenities for guests include two pools, boat ramp and slips, fishing docks, and tennis courts.

- $$
- 83 Units
- One-, two-, and three-bedroom apartments with fully equipped kitchens
- Pool
- Color Cable TV
- Guest Laundry
- Grills
- Handicapped Access
- Shuffleboard
- Pets (dogs under 20 pounds)
- Fax Services
- Mastercard, VISA, Discover
- Check-in: 2 P.M. Check-out: 10 A.M.

Resort Rental Communities

Manasota Key Realty, Inc.
Englewood
(941) 474-9536
(941) 474-2112 (fax)
(800) 881-9534

Points of Interest

Englewood Recreation Center
101 Orange Street
Englewood
(941) 474-8919
Beautiful recreation center offering lighted tennis and basketball courts, sandpit volleyball, playground, and picnic area with grills. The indoor facility has a fitness room and a game room.
Hours: 6 A.M. to 12 P.M.
Admission: Free

Indian Mound Park
210 Winson Avenue
Englewood
(941) 474-8919
This scenic park is home to a Calusa Indian Mound containing artifacts from 400 B.C.
Hours: 6 A.M. to 12 P.M.
Admission: Free

Lemon Bay Park & Environmental Center
5700 Bay Park Boulevard
Englewood
(941) 474-3065
Encompasses 187 acres on the Bay with nature displays, butterfly garden, nature trail, and picnic sites.
Hours: 8 A.M. to 12 A.M.
Admission: Free

Pelican Pete's Playland, Inc.
3101 South McCall
Englewood
(941) 475-2008
Miniature golf, arcade games, and go-carts

Dining Out

Barnacle Bill's Restaurant
1599 South McCall Road
Englewood
(941) 474-9703
Hours: 11 A.M. to 9 P.M.; Friday and Saturday until 10 P.M.
Features: fresh seafood, sandwiches, soups; casual dress; friendly service
Lunch: $3.95 to $6.95
Dinner: $11.95 to $18.95

Flying Bridge II Restaurant
2080 South McCall Road
Englewood
(941) 474-2206
Hours: 11 A.M. to 9 P.M.
Features: seafood, steak, children's menu, early bird specials; casual waterfront dining; outdoor patio
Lunch: $4 to $6
Dinner: $7 to $12

New Captain's Club Restaurant
1855 Gulf Boulevard
Englewood
(941) 475-8611
Hours: 11 A.M. to 10 P.M.; closed Tuesdays in the summer
Features: fresh seafood, steak; entertainment; casual waterfront dining with indoor bar and dockside tiki bar
Lunch: $3.95 to $7.95
Dinner: $9.95 to $22.95

Boca Grande

Accommodations

✍ Sea Oats of Boca Grande
5700 Gulf Shores Drive
Boca Grande, FL 33921
(941) 964-2080
(941) 964-0825 (fax)
(800) 962-3314

All units at Sea Oats are fully furninshed, two-bedroom/two bath condominiums with screened balconies overlooking either the Gulf or the tropically landscaped courtyard and pool area. This beautiful condominium complex features two lighted tennis courts, spacious sun decks, and covered parking. A seven-night minimum stay is required.

- TAC $$
- 87 Units
- Condominiums
- Pool
- Hot Tub
- Color Cable TV
- Guest Laundry
- Grills
- Handicapped Access
- Fax Services
- No Credit Cards
- Check-in: 3 P.M. Check-out: 10 A.M.

Resort Rental Companies

Boca Grande Real Estate, Inc.
Boca Grande
(941) 964-0338
(941) 964-2301 (fax)
(800) 881-2622

Sea Oats

Parsley-Baldwin Realty
Boca Grande
(800) 741-3074
e-mail: boca-pros@ewol.com
http://www.ewol.com/~re/boca-pros/index.htm

The Seale Family, Inc.
Boca Grande
(941) 964-2210
(941) 964-0474 (fax)
(800) 741-8272

Points of Interest

Boca Grande Community Center
Corner of Park Avenue and First Street
Boca Grande
(941) 964-2564
Two lighted tennis courts, basketball and volleyball courts, playground, and fitness center. Open to the public

Gasparilla Island State Recreation Area
(located at the south end of Gasparilla Island)

Dining Out

The Fishery Restaurant
Route 775 and Route 771
Placida
(941) 697-2451
Hours: 11:30 A.M. to 9:30 P.M.
Features: fresh seafood, sandwiches; casual Old Florida style waterfront dining
Lunch: $4.95 to $17.95
Dinner: $4.95 to $17.95

South Beach Restaurant
777 Gulf Boulevard
Boca Grande
(941) 964-0765
Hours: 11 A.M. to 2 A.M.
Features: fresh seafood, steak, homemade desserts; casual beach front dining; live entertainment
Lunch: $1.25 to $18.95
Dinner: $5.95 to $18.95

The Theater Restaurant
321 Park Avenue
Boca Grande
(941) 964-0614
Hours: 11 A.M. to 2:30 P.M., 5:30 P.M. to 9:30 P.M.; Sunday brunch, 11:30 A.M. to 2:30 P.M.
Features: seafood, steak, children's menu; casual and eclectic dining in a unique setting
Lunch: $4.95 to $24.95
Dinner: $4.95 to $24.95

SARASOTA/MANATEE AREA GOLF
(Semi-Private and Public)

Bird Bay Executive Golf Course
602 Bird Bay Drive West
Venice
(941) 485-9333
Semi-private

Bobby Jones Golf Complex
1000 Azinger Way
Sarasota
(941) 955-8097
Public; driving range, restaurant

Calusa Lakes Golf Course
1995 Calusa Lakes Boulevard
Nokomis
(941) 484-8995
Semi-private; driving range, restaurant

Capri Isles Golf Course
849 Capri Isles Boulevard
Venice
(941) 485-3371
Semi-private; driving range, restaurant

Boca Royale Country Club
1601 Englewood Road
Englewood
(941) 474-7475
Semi-private; driving range, restaurant

Gulf Gate Golf Club
2550 Bispham Road
Sarasota
(941) 921-5515
Semi-private; three nine-hole courses, restaurant

Jacaranda West Golf Course
601 Jacaranda Boulevard
Venice
(941) 493-2664
Semi-private; driving range, restaurant

Lake Venice Golf Course
South Harbor Drive
Venice
(941) 488-3948
Public; driving range

Manatee County Golf Course
6415 53rd Avenue West
Bradenton
(941) 792-6773
Public; driving range

Myakka Pines Golf Course
2550 South River Road
Englewood
(941) 474-3296
Semi-private; three nine-hole courses, driving range, restaurant

Palma Sola Golf Course
3807 75th Street West
Bradenton
(941) 792-7476
Public

Port Charlotte Golf Course
22400 Gleneagles Terrace
Port Charlotte
(941) 625-2334
Semi-private; driving range

Rolling Green Golf Course
4501 North Tuttle Avenue
Sarasota
(941) 355-6620
Semi-private; driving range, restaurant

Sabal Trace Golf Course
5456 Greenwood Avenue
North Port
(941) 426-2712
Semi-private; driving range, restaurant

Sorrento Par 3 Golf Course
1910 Bayshore Road
Nokomis
(941) 966-4884
Nine-hole, par 3

Village Green Golf Course
3500 Pembrook Drive
Sarasota
(941) 922-9500
Semi-private; restaurant

Stoneybrook Golf & Country Club
8801 Stoneybrook Boulevard
Sarasota
(941) 966-1800
Semi-private; driving range

Waterford Golf Course
1454 Gleneagles Drive
Venice
(941) 484-6621
Semi-private; driving range

Timber Creek Golf Course
4550 Timber Lane
Bradenton
(941) 794-8381
Nine-hole, par 27

CHAMBERS OF COMMERCE

Anna Maria Island Chamber of Commerce
PO Box 1892
Holmes Beach, FL 34218
(941) 778-1541

Bradenton Area Convention and Visitors Bureau
PO Box 1000
Bradenton, FL 34206
(941) 729-9177
(800) 4-MANATEE

Boca Grande Chamber of Commerce
Box 704
Boca Grande, FL 33921
(941) 964-0568

Englewood Area Chamber of Commerce
601 South Indiana Avenue
Englewood, FL 34223
(941) 474-5511

Longboat Key Chamber of Commerce
The Centre
5360 Gulf of Mexico Drive
Longboat Key, FL 34228
(941) 383-2466

Manatee Chamber of Commerce
222 Tenth Street West
Bradenton, FL 34205
(941) 748-3411

Sarasota Convention and Visitors Bureau
655 North Tamiami Trail
Sarasota, FL 34236
(941) 957-1877
(800) 522-9799

Siesta Key Chamber of Commerce
5263 Ocean Boulevard
Sarasota, FL 34242
(941) 349-3800

Venice Area Chamber of Commerce
257 North Tamiami Trail
Venice, FL 34285
(941) 488-2236

Southwest Beaches

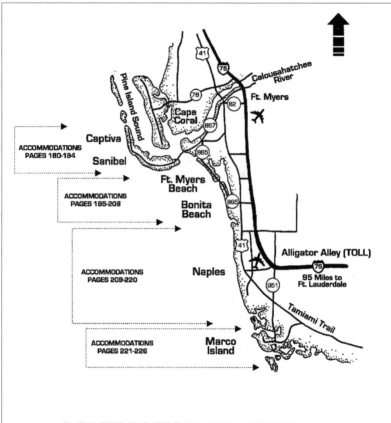

ACCOMMODATIONS
PAGES 180-194

Captiva

Sanibel

ACCOMMODATIONS
PAGES 195-208

Ft. Myers
Beach

Bonita
Beach

ACCOMMODATIONS
PAGES 209-220

Naples

ACCOMMODATIONS
PAGES 221-226

Marco
Island

Pine Island Sound

Cape
Coral

Ft. Myers

Calousahatchee
River

Alligator Alley (TOLL)

95 Miles to
Ft. Lauderdale

Tamiami Trail

SOUTHWEST BEACHES

SCALE IN MILES

Overview

Southwest Florida offers many charming, slow-paced beachfront communities including Sanibel, Captiva, Fort Myers Beach, Bonita Beach, Naples (including Vanderbilt Beach), and Marco Island. The Gulf of Mexico's warm waters, the sugary white sand beaches, and the lush tropical landscape create a beautiful vacation setting.

Located just over the Sanibel Causeway ($3 toll) is Sanibel, known worldwide for its beautiful beaches littered with more than 200 varieties of shells. Visitors spend hours looking for those perfect shells and soon develop the posture referred to as the "Sanibel Stoop." The island's beaches, with their natural setting, transports visitors to a world where life is reduced to the basics: sun, sea, sand, sky, and shells. Bike paths follow most of the major roads, making bicycling a nice way to get around the island. More than 30 miles of paved trails cover the islands and provide a great opportunity to see some of the beautiful plants and wildlife. Colorful shops, galleries, restaurants, and theaters line Periwinkle Way, one of Sanibel's main streets.

Captiva is just minutes north of Sanibel across Blind Pass Bridge. Captiva is very laidback, with a few restaurants, shops, and an old general store. Local marinas are nearby, offering a wide variety of watersport rentals including jet skis and kayaks. South Seas Plantation occupies the north end of Captiva Island. Although this is a gate-secured resort community, visitors are free to browse the shops and Captiva History House Museum.

Fort Myers Beach entices thousands of visitors each year. Situated on Estero Island off the coast of Fort Myers, this beach community cultivates a laidback family atmosphere. The island is a mere half mile wide and seven miles long. Here you can have it all. Fishermen will enjoy the five-hundred foot pier that juts into the Gulf at Lynn Hall Memorial Park on the northern end of the island. For water sports adventurers, windsurfing, parasailing, jet skiing, and water skiing are available. If shopping is your bag, try browsing the many fine boutiques for that special something. And when you've worked up an appetite, indulge yourself in some great seafood at one of the many restaurants.

Bonita Beach, just south of Fort Myers Beach, typifies Southwest Florida charm. The crystal blue Gulf and its beautiful beaches give an aura of quiet and comfort to those who visit.

Naples and Vanderbilt Beach offer visitors seven miles of white, sandy beaches. Predominantly residential in nature, the beaches here tend to be very quiet. The Naples area is rich in culture and boasts many fine galleries and a variety of performing arts events. The well-known Fifth   Avenue and Third Street shopping districts provide posh shops and restaurants.

Marco Island is just a short drive from Naples. Here you will find beautiful beaches with somewhat coarser sand that is excellent for shelling. Nature abounds and a variety of protected birds can be seen along the shoreline. More than seventy-five restaurants offer diversified cuisine. Golf is easy to find here as the Naples/Marco Island area has more golf courses per capita than any other metropolitan area in the country.

Climate

(Temperature by Degrees Farenheight)

SEASON	AVERAGE LOW	AVERAGE HIGH	GULF WATER
January–March	52	79	60s–70s
April–June	62	90	70s–80s
July–September	73	91	80s
October–December	54	85	60s–70s

Getting There

By Air

Naples Municipal Airport
(941) 643-0733
Location: 2 miles northeast of Naples

Southwest Florida International Airport
Fort Myers
(941) 768-1000
Location: 10 miles southeast of Fort Myers

By Car

INTERSTATE 75: From I-75 traveling north or south, west on Exit 21 (Daniels Parkway to Summerlin Road) for Sanibel and Captiva Islands and North Fort Myers Beach; west on Exit 18 (Bonita Beach Road) for South Fort Myers Beach and Bonita Beach; west on Exit 17 (Imomokalee Road to 111th Avenue) for Vanderbilt Beach; and west on Exit 16 (Pine Ridge Road to Seagate Drive or Crayton Road) for north and south Naples beaches.

INTERSTATE 95: If you are driving north via Jacksonville, take I-95 South to I-4, I-4 to I-75, and then south toward Naples. Follow directions for I-75 (above).

Sanibel/Captiva

Accommodations

 Beachview Cottages
3325 West Gulf Drive
Sanibel, FL 33957
(941) 472-1202
(941) 472-4720 (fax)
(800) 860-0532

Beachview Cottages offers quaint one- and two-bedroom old Florida style accommodations.

- TAC $$$
- 22 Units
- Cottages
- Pool
- Color Cable TV
- Guest Laundry
- Grills
- Fax Services
- Mastercard, VISA, Discover, American Express
- Check-in: 3 P.M. Check-out: 11 A.M.

Beachview Cottages

⚭ Blue Dolphin

4227 West Gulf Drive
Sanibel, FL 33957
(941) 472-1600
(941) 472-8615 (fax)
(800) 648-4660

Located in an exclusive residential area, the Blue Dolphin sits on a beautiful secluded beach. Complimentary beach chairs, umbrellas, and bicycles are available for guests.

- $$/$$$
- 9 Units
- Efficiencies with fully equipped kitchens
- Color Cable TV
- Guest Laundry
- Grills
- Handicapped Access
- Fax Services
- Mastercard, VISA
- Check-in: 2 P.M. Check-out: 10 A.M.

⚭ Caribe Beach Resort

2669 West Gulf Drive
Sanibel, FL 33957
(941) 472-1166
(941) 472-0079 (fax)
(800) 330-1593 (Kenoyer Real Estate)

Nestled among a grove of Australian pines, beautiful Caribe Beach Resort features large units, all with decks or balconies and most facing the pool or the grove.

- TAC $$$
- 26 Units
- Efficiencies; one-bedroom apartments with fully equipped kitchens; cottages
- Pool
- Hot Tub
- Color Cable TV
- Guest Laundry
- Grills
- Handicapped Access
- Shuffleboard
- Pets (1 per unit; under 25 pounds)
- Fax Services
- Mastercard, VISA
- Check-in: 3 P.M. Check-out: 10 A.M.

🐚 Holiday Inn Beach Resort

1231 Middle Gulf Drive
Sanibel, FL 33957
(941) 472-4123
(941) 472-0930 (fax)
(800) 443-0909

The Holiday Inn Beach Resort features ninety-eight guest rooms, including Gulf-view, suites, and standard rooms. Complimentary beach cabanas and tennis are available for guests.

- TAC $$$
- 98 Units
- Motel rooms and one-bedroom apartments with fully equipped kitchens
- Pool
- Color Cable TV
- Guest Laundry
- Handicapped Access
- Restaurant/Bar
- Conference Facilities
- Fax Services
- Mastercard, VISA, Discover, American Express
- Check-in: 3 P.M. Check-out: 11 A.M.

🐚 Mitchell's Sand Castles

3951 West Gulf Drive
Sanibel, FL 33957
(941) 472-1282

These cute gray-and-white rustic cottages are located in a quiet, residential area. Most have porches and some have a beach view.

- $$/$$$
- 18 Units
- One-, two- and three-bedroom apartments with fully equipped kitchens; cottages
- Pool
- Color Cable TV
- Guest Laundry
- Grills
- Handicapped Access
- Pets ($5 per stay)
- No Credit Cards
- Check-in: 2 P.M. Check-out: 10 A.M.

☜ Sanibel Beach Club II

205 Periwinkle Way
Sanibel, FL 33957
(941) 472-5772
(941) 472-3790 (fax)

Eight separate, two-story buildings all centered around a lushly land-scaped pool area comprise the grounds of the Sanibel Beach Club II. All rooms face the Gulf and have a washer and dryer. Covered parking is available under each unit.

- $$/$$$
- 29 Units
- Two-bedroom apartments with fully equipped kitchens
- Pool
- Hot Tub
- Color Cable TV
- Guest Laundry
- Grills
- Shuffleboard
- Fax Services
- Mastercard, VISA, Discover
- Check-in: 3 P.M. Check-out: 10 A.M.

☜ Sanibel Inn

937 East Gulf Drive
Sanibel, FL 33957
(941) 472-3181
(941) 472-5234 (fax)
(800) 237-1491

The Sanibel Inn features two-story, pastel-colored buildings. All units have a small refrigerator, microwave, coffee maker, toaster, and private balconies facing the pool or Gulf. The two-bedroom condominiums have fully equipped kitchens and a washer and dryer.

- $$/$$$
- 96 Units
- Suites and two-bedroom condominiums
- Pool
- Color Cable TV
- Grills
- Handicapped Access
- Fax Services
- Mastercard, VISA, Discover, American Express
- Check-in: 3 P.M. Check-out: 11 A.M.

✍ Sanibel Moorings

845 East Gulf Drive
Sanibel, FL 33957
(941) 472-4119
(941) 472-8148 (fax)
(800) 237-5144

Sanibel Moorings offers one-, two- and three-bedroom condominiums situated on beautiful grounds with lots of exotic plants. The units have screened porches. Weekly rentals are preferred.

- TAC $$$
- 110 Units
- Condominiums
- Pool
- Color Cable TV
- Guest Laundry
- Grills
- Conference Facilities
- Fax Services
- Mastercard, VISA
- Check-in: 4:30 P.M. Check-out: 11 A.M.

Sanibel Moorings

Sanibel's Seaside Inn

⟨⟨⟨ Sanibel's Seaside Inn

541 East Gulf Drive
Sanibel, FL 33957
(941) 472-1400
(941) 472-6518 (fax)
(800) 831-7384

The Seaside Inn is a small, cozy resort with quaint pastel accommodations nestled amid towering palms and native flowers. Newly renovated one-, two- and three-bedroom suites and cottages have their own private porches or balconies. Bicycles and beach chairs are complimentary for guests, as well as a continental breakfast basket delivered daily to your room.

- TAC $$$
- 32 Units
- One-, two-, and three-bedroom apartments with fully equipped kitchens; cottages
- Pool
- Color Cable TV
- Guest Laundry
- Grills
- Shuffleboard
- Fax Services
- Mastercard, VISA, Discover, American Express
- Check-in: 2 P.M. Check-out: 11 A.M.

☞ Shalimar Resort

2823 West Gulf Drive
Sanibel, FL 33957
(941) 472-1353
(941) 472-6430 (fax)
(800) 472-1353

Individual housekeeping cottages with tin roofs and screened porches create an old Florida atmosphere at the Shalimar Resort.

- $$$
- 33 Units
- Efficiencies; two-bedroom apartments with fully equipped kitchens; cottages
- Pool
- Color Cable TV
- Guest Laundry
- Handicapped Access
- Shuffleboard
- Fax Services
- Mastercard, VISA, Discover
- Check-in: 2 P.M. Check-out: 11 A.M.

☞ Shell Island Beach Club

255 Periwinkle Way
Sanibel, FL 33957
(941) 472-4497
(941) 472-4218 (fax)
(800) 448-2736 (Hilton Grand Vacation Rentals Reservations)

Shell Island Beach Club has luxurious two-bedroom condominiums with washers and dryers, VCRs, and screened porches. Tennis courts and bicycles are available. Weekly rentals are preferred.

Shalimar Resort

Shell Island Beach Club

- $$$
- 56 Units
- Condominiums
- Pool
- Hot Tub
- Color Cable TV
- Guest Laundry

- Grills
- Handicapped Access
- Fax Services
- Mastercard, VISA, Discover, American Express
- Check-in: 3 P.M. Check-out: 10 A.M.

⚭ Snook Motel

3033 West Gulf Drive
Sanibel, FL 33957
(941) 472-1345
(941) 472-2148 (fax)
(800) 741-6166

The Snook Motel offers modern, spacious accommodations with private balconies or screened porches. Most units have kitchens, and daily maid service is provided.

- $$/$$$
- 27 Units
- Motel rooms; efficiencies with fully equipped kitchens; cottages
- Pool
- Color Cable TV

- Guest Laundry
- Grills
- Shuffleboard
- Fax Services
- Mastercard, VISA, Discover, American Express
- Check-in: 2 P.M. Check-out: 11 A.M.

⚭ Song of the Sea

863 East Gulf Drive
Sanibel, FL 33957
(941) 472-2220
(941) 472-8569 (fax)
(800) 231-1045

Song of the Sea combines the charming intimacy of a European inn with the lush tropics of Southwest Florida. All units have screened patios. Complimentary fresh flowers and wine greet your arrival, and a daily continental breakfast is provided. Bicycles and beach umbrellas are also complimentary.

- TAC $$$
- 30 Units
- Suites and efficiencies with fully equipped kitchens
- Pool
- Hot Tub
- Color Cable TV
- Guest Laundry
- Grills
- Shuffleboard
- Fax Services
- Mastercard, VISA, Discover, American Express
- Check-in: 3 P.M. Check-out: 11 A.M.

⬆ Stafford on the Beach (American Realty)

PO Box 1133
Captiva, FL 33926
(941) 472-0564
(941) 472-3284 (fax)
(800) 547-0127

Stafford on the Beach is a private home featuring three bedrooms, two bathrooms, two screened porches, a large great room, and a new kitchen. The home offers beautiful views of sunsets over the Gulf of Mexico.

- TAC $$$
- 1 Unit
- Private home
- Hot Tub
- Color Cable TV
- Guest Laundry
- Grills
- Fax Services
- Mastercard, VISA
- Check-in: 2 P.M. Check-out: 10 A.M.

⬆ Tortuga Beach Club

959 East Gulf Drive
Sanibel, FL 33957
(941) 472-0400
(941) 472-6540 (fax)
(800) 448-2736 (Hilton Grande Vacations Rentals Reservations)

Tortuga Beach Club is a tropical paradise with two-bedroom townhouses that sleep up to six people. Designer furnishings and screened balconies make it the perfect environment for a peaceful getaway. Amenities also include limited golf membership, four tennis courts, volleyball, and a recreational program.

- TAC $$$
- 54 Units
- Townhouses
- Pool
- Hot Tub
- Color Cable TV
- Guest Laundry
- Grills
- Shuffleboard
- Fax Services
- Mastercard, VISA, Discover, American Express
- Check-in: 3 P.M. Check-out: 10 A.M.

Tortuga Beach Club

Resort Rental Companies

American Realty of Captiva
Captiva
(941) 472-0564
(941) 472-3284 (fax)
(800) 547-0127

Grande Island Vacations
Sanibel
(941) 472-5322
(941) 472-5722 (fax)
(800) 551-7788

Sanibel Accommodations
Sanibel
(941) 472-3191
(941) 472-4519 (fax)
(800) 237-6004

Points of Interest

Bailey-Matthews Shell Museum
3075 Sanibel-Captiva Road
Sanibel
(941) 395-2233
The only museum in the country devoted to shells
Hours: 10 A.M. to 4 P.M. daily except Mondays
Admission: Adults, $5; children ages 8 to 16, $3; children 7 and under, free

J. N. "Ding" Darling National Wildlife Refuge
1 Wildlife Drive
Sanibel
(941) 472-1100
A wilderness preserve with 5,030 acres of nature trails, five-mile scenic drive, and canoe trails showing Florida wildlife in its natural habitat.

Hours: 7:30 A.M. to 7 P.M. daily except Fridays
Admission: In a car: $4 per car; on foot or bike: $1 per family

Sanibel Historical Museum
950 Dunlop Road
Sanibel
(941) 472-4648
Displays and exhibits explaining the history of Sanibel Island from the days of the Calusa Indians
Hours: Wednesday through Saturday, 10 A.M. to 4 P.M.
Admission: $2 donation

Sanibel Lighthouse (located on Sanibel's southern tip)
The lighthouse has been a landmark since 1884.

Sanibel/Captiva Nature Conservation
(located at Mile Marker One on Sanibel-Captiva Road)
(941) 472-2329
A 247-acre wetlands area offering over four miles of nature trails.
Hours: Seasonal; call for hours
Admission: Adults, $3; children under 17, free

Dining Out

The Bubble Room
15001 Captiva Drive
Captiva
(941) 472-5558
Hours: 11:30 A.M. to 2:30 P.M.; 5 P.M. to 10 P.M.
Features: seafood, steak, children's menu, hearty portions, great desserts; proper casual attire; brimming with 1930s and '40s memorabilia
Lunch: $5.95 to $11.95
Dinner: $13.95 to $26.95

Gramma Dots
634 North Yachtsman
Sanibel Marina

(941) 472-8138
Hours: 11:30 A.M. to 7:30 P.M.
Features: great seafood, chicken, burgers, children's menu; casual dockside dining
Lunch: $3.25 to $12.95
Dinner: $12.95 to $19.95 (lunch menu is available after 5 P.M. for a $1 additional charge)

Green Flash Bayside Bar and Grill
(located half mile south of Andy Rose Lane)
Overlooking Pine Island Sound
Captiva
(941) 472-3337
Hours: 11:30 A.M. to 2:30 P.M.; 5:30 P.M. to 9:30 P.M.
Features: seafood, chicken, steak, children's menu; casual waterfront dining; arrive by car or boat
Lunch: $2.95 to $9.95
Dinner: $12.95 to $27.95

The Jacaranda
1223 Periwinkle Way
Sanibel
(941) 472-1771
Hours: 5 P.M. to 10 p.m; bar open until 12:30 A.M.
Features: seafood, steak, pasta, children's menu, early bird specials; casual dining; outdoor dining available; live entertainment
Dinner: $14.95 to $19.95

Lighthouse Cafe
362 PeriwinkleWay
Sanibel
(941) 472-0303
Hours: 7 A.M. to 3 P.M.
Features: seafood, steak, pasta; great breakfast served all day; dinner served mid-December through Easter; casual attire
Breakfast: $2.95 to $5.95
Lunch: $3.85 to $5.95

The Mucky Duck
Andy Rosse Lane
Captiva
(941) 472-3434
Hours: 11:30 A.M. to 2:30 P.M.; 5 P.M. to 9:30 P.M.
Features: homemade New England Chowder, roasted duckling, hefty sandwiches, homemade key lime pie, children's menu; casual waterfront English pub; non-smoking restaurant
Lunch: $2.50 to $9.95
Dinner: $11.98 to $18.96

Fort Myers Beach/Bonita Beach

Accommodations

🐚 Bahama Beach Club Condominiums

5370 Estero Boulevard
Ft. Myers Beach, FL 33931
(941) 463-3148

The Bahama Beach Club has beautifully furnished one- and two-bedroom condominiums that resemble the old Florida style.

- $$$
- 22 Units
- Condominiums
- Pool
- Color Cable TV

- Guest Laundry
- Grills
- Mastercard, VISA
- Check-in: 3 P.M. Check-out: 10 A.M.

🐚 Beach House Motel

26106 Hickory Boulevard
Bonita Beach, FL 34134
(941) 992-2644
(941) 992-2644 (fax)

Newly renovated, the Beach House has eight individual buildings with apartments upstairs and downstairs. The upstairs apartments have screened porches.

- $$
- 48 Units
- Motel rooms; one- and two-bedroom apartments with fully equipped kitchens

- Color Cable TV
- Grills
- Mastercard, VISA
- Check-in: 3 P.M. Check-out: 10 A.M.

☯ Beacon Motel

1240 Estero Boulevard
Ft. Myers Beach, FL 33931
(941) 463-5264
(941) 463-5972 (fax)

This family owned and operated motel offers updated and very clean rooms. A gift shop is on the property. The Beacon Motel has Gulf-view efficiencies and one beachfront cottage.

- TAC $$
- 14 Units
- Motel rooms; one-bedroom apartments with fully equipped kitchens; one cottage
- Color Cable TV
- Guest Laundry
- Grills
- Mastercard, VISA, Discover, American Express
- Check-in: 3 P.M. Check-out: 10 A.M.

☯ Best Western Beach Resort

684 Estero Boulevard
Ft. Myers Beach, FL 33931
(941) 463-6000
(941) 463-3013 (fax)
(800) 336-4045

The Best Western Beach Resort has efficiencies that all face the Gulf. The lush, tropical landscape is gorgeous.

- TAC $$$
- 75 Units
- Efficiencies with fully equipped kitchens
- Pool
- Color Cable TV
- Guest Laundry
- Grills
- Shuffleboard
- Pets (under 25 pounds; $15 per stay)
- Fax Services
- Mastercard, VISA, Discover, American Express
- Check-in: 3 P.M. Check-out: 11 A.M.

Beacon Motel

Best Western Beach Resort

☞ Best Western Pink Shell Beach Resort

275 Estero Boulevard
Ft. Myers Beach, FL 33931
(941) 463-6181
(941) 463-1229 (fax)
(800) 237-5786

The Pink Shell is the largest full-service resort on Fort Myers Beach, with twelve acres of tropical paradise and 1500 feet of sugary white sand beach. Four tennis courts are available for guests.

- TAC $$$
- 208 Units
- Suites; efficiencies with fully equipped kitchens; cottages
- Pool
- Color Cable TV
- Guest Laundry
- Grills
- Handicapped Access
- Restaurant/Bar
- Shuffleboard
- Conference Facilities
- Fax Services
- Mastercard, VISA, Discover, American Express
- Check-in: 4 P.M. Check-out: 11 A.M.

☞ Buccaneer Resort Inn

4864 Estero Boulevard
Ft. Myers Beach, FL 33931
(941) 463-5728
(941) 463-5756 (fax)

The Buccaneer Resort Inn is family owned and operated and has nicely furnished, spotless rooms.

- TAC $$/$$$
- 28 Units
- Motel rooms, efficiencies, and two-bedroom apartments with fully equipped kitchens
- Pool
- Color Cable TV
- Guest Laundry
- Grills
- Shuffleboard
- Fax Services
- Mastercard, VISA, Discover, American Express
- Check-in: 3 P.M. Check-out: 10 A.M.

Buccaneer Resort Inn

✍ Lani Kai Island Resort

1400 Estero Boulevard
Fort Myers Beach, FL 33931
(941) 463-3111
(941) 463-2986 (fax)
(800) 237-6133
http://www.drfun.com/lani-kai.htm

The Lani Kai has private balconies all facing the Gulf and private beach. Other amenities include a gift shop, salon, daycare, playground, three beach bars, and a beach nightclub with live entertainment from 2 P.M. to 2 A.M. This is a hot spot for many "Spring Breakers."

- TAC $$$
- 100 Units
- Motel rooms; one- and two-bedroom apartments with fully equipped kitchens
- Pool
- Color TV

- Guest Laundry
- Handicapped Access
- Restaurant/Bar
- Conference facilities
- Fax Services
- Mastercard, VISA, Discover
- Check-in: 3 P.M. Check-out: 11 A.M.

Lani Kai Island Resort

🌊 Outrigger Beach Resort
6200 Estero Boulevard
Fort Myers Beach, FL 33931
(941) 463-3131
(941) 463-6577 (fax)
(800) 749-3131
http://www.outriggerfmb.com

The Outrigger Beach Resort is a casual beachfront resort. Approximately half of the 144 units are efficiencies. The Deckside Cafe provides guests with, among many other meals, a choice of fresh seafood. The Tiki Bar is well known for its sunset conch yell. Daily activities, weekly wine and cheese parties, and live entertainment make this a nice vacation destination.

- TAC $$$
- 144 Units
- Motel rooms and efficiencies
  with fully equipped kitchens
- Pool
- Color Cable TV
- Guest Laundry
- Grills

- Handicapped Access
- Restaurant/Bar
- Shuffleboard
- Fitness Center
- Conference Facilities
- Fax Services
- Mastercard, VISA, Discover
- Check-in: 2 P.M. Check-out: 11 A.M.

ॐ Pointe Estero

6640 Estero Boulevard
Ft. Myers Beach, FL 33931
(941) 765-1155
(941) 765-0657 (fax)
(800) 237-5141

The two-bedroom condominiums at Pointe Estero are beautifully decorated and have screened balconies overlooking the Gulf. The units all come with a washer and dryer, a TV in every room, and a Jacuzzi tub in the master bathroom. Tennis is available for guests.

- $$$
- 60 Units
- Condominiums
- Pool
- Hot Tub
- Color Cable TV
- Guest Laundry
- Grills
- Handicapped Access
- Fax Services
- Mastercard, VISA, Discover
- Check-in: 3 P.M.
  Check-out: 10 A.M.

Pointe Estero

℘ Porpoise Pass Motel

26210 Hickory Boulevard
Bonita Beach, FL 34134
(941) 947-1997

Porpoise Pass Motel is an old Florida style resort with modern conveniences. You can walk across the street to a great deli and general store.

- $$
- 13 Units
- One-bedroom apartments with fully equipped kitchens
- Color Cable TV
- Guest Laundry
- Grills
- Pets (small pets accepted at owner's discretion, no fee)
- Mastercard, VISA
- Check-in: 1 P.M. Check-out: 10 A.M.

Porpoise Pass Motel on the Beach

⬦ Sandpiper Gulf Resort

5550 Estero Boulevard
Ft. Myers Beach, FL 33931
(941) 463-5721
(941) 463-5721 (fax)

The Sandpiper offers comfortable and luxurious accommodations that are tastefully appointed as well as functionally designed. The living area converts for sleeping, and the large bedroom area has two double beds and a generous closet. All rooms have private balconies.

- $$
- 63 Units
- Efficiencies with fully equipped kitchens
- Pool
- Hot Tub
- Color Cable TV
- Guest Laundry
- Grills
- Handicapped Access
- Shuffleboard
- Fax Services
- Mastercard, VISA, Discover
- Check-in: 2 P.M. Check-out: 11 A.M.

⬦ Tiki Resort Motel

4360 Estero Boulevard
Ft. Myers Beach, FL 33931
(941) 463-9547

The Tiki Resort Motel has 2 two-story buildings with a Key West tropical flair. The rooms are clean, and most have screened porches.

- $$
- 10 Units
- One-bedroom apartments with fully equipped kitchens
- Color Cable TV
- Guest Laundry
- Grills
- No Credit Cards
- Check-in: 2 P.M. Check-out: 10 A.M.

✍ Tropical Inn Resort Motel

5210 Estero Boulevard
Ft. Myers Beach, FL 33931
(941) 463-3124
(941) 463-0417 (fax)

The Tropical Inn Resort offers clean rooms in a three-story building with balconies overlooking the pool and Gulf.

- $$
- 28 Units
- Efficiencies with fully equipped kitchens
- Pool
- Color Cable TV
- Guest Laundry
- Grills
- Handicapped Access
- Fax Services
- Mastercard, VISA, American Express
- Check-in: 2 P.M. Check-out: 11 A.M.

✍ Windward Passage Resort

418 Estero Boulevard
Ft. Myers Beach, FL 33931
(941) 463-1194
(941) 463-1194 (fax)

The Windward Passage Resort offers exquisitely furnished one- and two-bedroom condominiums with screened balconies. The tropical pool area is nestled behind sea oats. Tennis and bicycles are available. There is a two-night minimum stay.

- TAC $$$
- 2 Units
- Condominiums
- Pool
- Hot Tub
- Color Cable TV
- Guest Laundry
- Grills
- Handicapped
- Shuffleboard
- Fax Services
- Mastercard, VISA, Discover
- Check-in: 3 P.M. Check-out: 10 A.M.

Windward Passage Resort

Points of Interest

Thomas Edison and Henry Ford Winter Homes
2350 McGregor Boulevard
Fort Myers
(941) 334-7419
Tour Edison's home, laboratory, and gardens. Ford's home is next door.
Hours: Monday through Saturday, 9 A.M. to 3:30 P.M.; Sunday, 12 P.M. to 3:30 P.M.
Admission: $10 for both tours; $8 for Edison's home only

Estero Bay Boat Tours, Inc.
5231 Mamie Street
Bonita Springs
(941) 992-2200
Take an afternoon, lunch, dinner, shelling, or sunset cruise on the Gulf of Mexico aboard the Horizons. Each 38-foot pontoon boat offers a scenic two-hour trip for up to 40 people.
Admission: Adults, $8; children under 12, $8

Everglades Wonder Gardens

27081 Old US 41

Downtown Bonita Springs

(941) 992-2591

Immerse yourself in lush tropical gardens while viewing the mammals, reptiles, and birds of the Everglades. Southwest Florida's oldest attraction

Hours: 9 A.M. to 5 P.M. daily; last tour at 4:15 P.M.

Admission: Adults, $9; children ages 3 to 12, $5; children 2 and under, free

Golf Safari

3775 Bonita Beach Road

Bonita Beach

(941) 947-1377

Miniature golf

Imaginarium Hands-On Science Museum and Aquarium

Cranford Avenue at Dr. Martin Luther King Jr. Boulevard

Fort Myers

(941) 337-3332

New attraction featuring interactive exhibits on the humanities and physical and aquatic sciences. Great for all ages

Hours: 10 A.M. to 5 P.M. daily except Mondays

Admission: Adults, $6; children ages 3 to 12, $3; children 2 and under, free

Carl Johnson Park

(located on County Road 865 on the causeway just north of Bonita Beach)

This 285-acre park, adjacent to Lover's Key, is densly vegetated with mangrove trees and is home to the American osprey, fiddler crab, and numerous sea birds.

Hours: 7 A.M. to sundown

Dining Out

Anthony's on the Gulf

3040 Estero Boulevard
Fort Myers Beach
(941) 463-2600
Hours: 11:30 A.M. to 10 P.M.; Friday and Saturday until 11 P.M.
Features: seafood, pasta, sandwiches, children's menu; casual beachfront dining
Lunch: $5 to $9
Dinner: $9 to $19

The Beach Pierside Grill

1000 Estero Boulevard (next to public pier)
Fort Myers Beach
(941) 765-7800
Hours: 11 A.M. to 11 P.M.
Features: sandwiches, seafood; casual waterfront dining; outside patio; happy hour; entertainment
Lunch: $4.95 to $14.95
Dinner: $4.95 to $14.95

Castaways Italian Village

(located across from Bonita Public Beach)
5900 Bonita Beach Road
Bonita Beach
(941) 947-3171
Hours: 11 A.M. to 9 P.M.
Features: Italian specialties, steak, seafood, children's menu, breakfast on Sundays from 8 A.M.
Lunch: $4.95 to $7.95
Dinner: $8.95 to $18.95

Channel Mark

19001 San Carlos Boulevard
Fort Myers Beach

(941) 463-9127
Hours: 11 A.M. to 10 P.M.; Friday and Saturday until 11 P.M.
Features: homemade pasta specialties, seafood; casual waterfront dining; live jazz entertainment on weekends; come by car or boat
Lunch: $4.95 to $9.95
Dinner: $9.95 to $24.95

Island Deli
26105 Hickory Boulevard
Bonita Beach
(941) 992-1112
Hours: 9 A.M. to 6 P.M.
Features: great sandwiches and friendly service; dine in or take out
Lunch: $2.95 to $5.95

Ro'des Seafood Market Restaurant
3998 Bonita Beach Road
Bonita Springs
(941) 992-4040
(800) 786-0450
Hours: 9 A.M. to 9 P.M.
Features: great prepared-to-order seafood, children's menu; casual dining
Lunch: $5.95 to $8.95
Dinner: $7.95 to $12.95

Rooftop Restaurant/Flying Fish Cafe
25999 Hickory Boulevard
Bonita Springs
(941) 992-0033
Hours: 5 P.M. to 10 P.M.
Features: Sunday brunch, seafood, steak; smartly casual dining; piano bar nightly; supervised children's play area
Dinner: $12.95 to $39.95
Flying Fish Cafe is open from 11:30 A.M. to 8 P.M. and offers outside or indoor casual dining. Menu prices range from $6.95 to $19.95.

Naples

Accommodations

Edgewater Beach Hotel
1901 Gulf Shore Boulevard
Naples, FL 34102
(941) 403-2000
(941) 403-2100 (fax)
(800) 821-0196

The Edgewater Beach Hotel is an intimate, all-suite boutique beach resort. The suites are richly appointed and very well kept. The Edgewater is a distinguished member of Insignia Resorts, a worldwide consortium of the finest luxury. The hotel received a Four Diamond rating by the American Automobile Association.

- TAC $$$
- 124 Units
- One- and two-bedroom suites
- Pool
- Color Cable TV
- Guest Laundry
- Handicapped Access
- Restaurant/Bar
- Shuffleboard
- Fitness Center
- Conference Facilities
- Fax Services
- Mastercard, VISA, Discover, American Express
- Check-in: 3 P.M. Check-out: 12 P.M.

LaPlaya Beach Resort
9891 Gulf Shore Drive
Naples, FL 34108
(941) 597-3123
(941) 597-8283 (fax)
(800) 237-6883

LaPlaya Beach Resort offers 191 spacious guest rooms, all with private balconies and Gulf views.

- TAC $$$
- 191 Units
- Hotel rooms
- Pool
- Color Cable TV
- Guest Laundry
- Handicapped Access
- Restaurant/Bar
- Fitness Center
- Conference Facilities
- Fax Services
- Mastercard, VISA, Discover, American Express
- Check-in: 4 P.M. Check-out: 12 P.M.

⬯ The Naples Beach Hotel & Golf Club
851 Gulf Shore Boulevard North
Naples, FL 34102
(941) 261-2222
(941) 261-7380 (fax)
(800) 237-7600
http://www.naplesbeachhotel.com

The Naples Beach Hotel & Golf Club

The Naples Beach Hotel & Golf Club is a huge resort with six tennis courts, an eighteen-hole championship golf course, five restaurants, gift shop, and complimentary "Beach Klub" for kids, all situated on 1000 feet of newly renourished beach.

- TAC $$$
- 318 Units
- Suites and efficiencies with fully equipped kitchens
- Pool
- Color Cable TV
- Handicapped Access
- Restaurant/Bar
- Conference Facilities
- Fax Services
- Mastercard, VISA, Discover, American Express
- Check-in: 4 P.M. Check-out: 12 P.M.

✆ The Registry Resort, Naples

475 Seagate Drive
Naples, FL 34103
(941) 597-3232
(941) 597-3147 (fax)
(800) 247-9810
http://www.registryhotels.com

The Registry Resort is a modern, majestic tower filled with luxurious, spacious guest rooms and suites overlooking 23 acres of a 200-acre lush tropical mangrove preserve. A complimentary tram ride takes you over a boardwalk through the mangrove preserve to the beach. This beautiful resort offers casual elegance, a variety of award-winning restaurants, golf, tennis, three pools, night club, and Camp Registry kids program for five- to twelve-year-olds. Although this hotel is six-tenths of a mile off the beach, I included it for its uniqueness and the friendly service that I encountered during my visit.

- TAC $$$
- 474 Units
- Hotel rooms and suites
- Pool
- Hot Tub
- Color Cable TV
- Guest Laundry
- Handicapped Access
- Restaurant/Bar
- Shuffleboard
- Fitness Center
- Conference Facilities
- Fax Services
- Mastercard, VISA, Discover, American Express
- Check-in: 3 P.M. Check-out: 12 P.M.

The Registry Resort, Naples

Boardwalk at The Registry Resort, Naples

☜ The Ritz-Carlton, Naples
280 Vanderbilt Beach Road
Naples, FL 34108
(941) 598-3300
(941) 598-6690 (fax)
(800) 241-3333

The Ritz-Carlton, Naples is the only Mobil Five-Star, AAA Five-Diamond luxury resort in Florida. Located amid the tropical splendor of Southwest Florida, the resort features three miles of beaches, six tennis courts, numerous water sports, bicycles, shopping, five restaurants, a night club, and nearby golf.

- $$$
- 463 Units
- Hotel rooms and suites
- Pool
- Hot Tub
- Color Cable TV
- Guest Laundry
- Handicapped Access
- Restaurant/Bar
- Fitness Center
- Conference Facilities
- Fax Services
- Mastercard, VISA, Discover, American Express
- Check-in: 3 P.M. Check-out: 12 P.M.

☜ The Tides Inn of Naples
1801 Gulf Shore Boulevard North
Naples, FL 34102
(941) 262-6196
(941) 262-3055 (fax)
(800) 438-8763

The Tides Inn offers every comfort of modern and luxurious living. The units are well-maintained inside and out, and have private screened porches overlooking the Gulf. Complimentary continental breakfast is available daily.

- TAC $$$
- 35 Units
- Hotel rooms; efficiencies; one- and two-bedroom apartments with fully equipped kitchens
- Pool
- Color Cable TV
- Guest Laundry
- Shuffleboard
- Fax Services
- Mastercard, VISA, American Express
- Check-in: 2 P.M. Check-out: 11 A.M.

⊗ Vanderbilt Beach & Harbour Club

9301 Gulf Shore Drive
Naples, FL 34108
(941) 597-6093
(941) 597-7216 (fax)
(800) 331-4941
e-mail: phaseiii@naples.infi.net

Vanderbilt Beach & Harbour Club offers elegance, luxury, and privacy in two-bedroom, two-bathroom condominiums. Spacious, airy, and well-appointed units are completely furnished and include a washer and dryer as well as a waterfront, screened balcony. The resort features two pools, sauna, bicycles, horeseshoes, and a Bayfront dock offering pontoon boat rentals.

Vanderbilt Beach & Harbour Club

- TAC $$$
- 44 Units
- Two-bedroom condominiums
- Pool
- Hot Tub
- Color Cable TV
- Guest Laundry

- Grills
- Shuffleboard
- Fitness Center
- Conference Facilities
- Fax Services
- Mastercard, VISA
- Check-in: 3 P.M. Check-out: 10 P.M.

⑳ Vanderbilt Beach Motel
9225 Gulfshore Drive North
Naples, FL 34108
(941) 597-3144
(941) 597-2199 (fax)
(800) 243-9076
http://www.bestof.net/naples/hotels/vbm

The Vanderbilt Beach Motel is situated on three acres of park-like grounds. The units are spacious and tastefully decorated and can accommodate up to six people. Enjoy unlimited tennis on the Omni surface court.

- $/$$/$$$
- 62 Units
- Motel rooms; one- and two-bedroom apartments with fully equipped kitchens
- Pool
- Color Cable TV
- Guest Laundry

- Grills
- Restaurant/Bar
- Shuffleboard
- Conference Facilities
- Fax Services
- Mastercard, VISA, Discover, American Express
- Check-in: 1 P.M. Check-out: 11 A.M.

⑳ Vanderbilt Inn on the Gulf
11000 Gulf Shore Drive North
Naples, FL 34108
(941) 597-3151
(941) 597-6075 (fax)
(800) 643-8654
http://www.bestof.net/naples/hotels/vanderbilt_inn/info.htm
e-mail: vandy@naples.net

Nestled away in a world of its own, this classic island-style resort offers 147 tropically decorated rooms, including sixteen Gulf-front efficiencies. The beach adjacent to the hotel was recognized as the eleventh best beach in the nation.

- TAC $$$
- 147 Units
- Motel rooms and efficiencies with fully equipped kitchens
- Pool
- Color Cable TV
- Guest Laundry
- Handicapped Access
- Restaurant/Bar
- Conference Facilities
- Fax Services
- Mastercard, VISA, Discover, American Express
- Check-in: 3 P.M. Check-out: 11 A.M.

⬮ Vanderbilt Vacation Villas
9467 Gulf Shore Drive
Naples, FL 34108
(941) 597-1141
(941) 597-1142 (fax)

The surroundings and lifestyle at the Vanderbilt Vacation Villas are casual.

- $$
- 22 Units
- Efficiencies and one-bedroom apartments with fully equipped kitchens
- Color Cable TV
- Grills
- Fax Services
- Mastercard, VISA
- Check-in: 2 P.M. Check-out: 10 A.M.

Resort Rental Companies

Bluebill Vacation Properties, Inc.
Naples
(941) 992-6620
(941) 992-9552 (fax)
(800) 237-2010
e-mail: info@bluebill.com
http://www.naplesvacation.com

Destinations Florida Marketing, Inc.
Naples
(941) 774-4445
(941) 774-1745 (fax)
e-mail: all-florida@naplesnet.com
http://www.all-florida.com

Points of Interest

Boardwalk Amusements
823 Vanderbilt Beach Road
Naples
(941) 597-1005
Features many popular video, skeeball, pinball, and basketball games.

The Conservancy's Briggs Nature Center
401 Shell Island Road
Naples
(941) 775-8569
This interpretive center features hands-on exhibits and large aquariums filled with mangrove-estuary inhabitants. A half-mile boardwalk leads visitors through five different ecosystems. Also features a butterfly garden filled with native plants designed to attract more than twenty-seven species of butterflies. Canoe and kayak rentals available
Hours: 9 A.M. to 4:30 P.M.
Admission: Adults, $3; children ages 6 to 18, $1; children 5 and under, free

Coral Cay Adventure Golf
2205 Tamiami Trail East
Naples
(941) 793-4999
Miniature golf

Jungle Larry's Caribbean Gardens

1590 Goodlette-Frank Road
Naples
(941) 262-5409
This attraction has a Florida panther, black leopard, Bengal tigers, sloths, monkeys, and other animals in natural habitats.
Hours: 9:30 A.M. to 5:30 P.M. daily
Admission: Adults, $13.95; children ages 4 to 15, $8.95; children 3 and under, free

King Richards Family Fun Center

6780 North Airport Road
Naples
(941) 598-1666
Medieval castle featuring one of Southwest Florida's largest go-cart tracks and arcades. Also has two miniature golf courses and batting cages

Naples Nature Center

1450 Merrihue Drive
Naples
(941) 262-0304
This center features the Natural Science Museum—home to snakes, seashells, and a giant fish tank—as well as the Wildlife Rehabilitation Center.
Hours: 9 A.M. to 4:30 P.M. daily except Sundays
Admission: Adults, $5; children ages 5 to 17, $1; children ages 4 and under, free

---

Dining Out

D'Amici's

11375 East Tamiami Trail
Naples
(941) 732-1600
Hours: 5:30 P.M. to 9:30 P.M.; closed in the summer

Features: great Italian specialties, children's menu; casual, romantic dining
Dinner: $9.95 to $14.95

HB's on the Gulf
(located in the Naples Beach Hotel)
851 Gulf Shore Boulevard
Naples
(941) 261-2222
Hours: 11:30 A.M. to 3 P.M., 5 P.M. to 10:30 P.M.
Features: fresh seafood, pasta, steak, sandwiches, vegetarian dishes; smartly casual outdoor or indoor dining
Lunch: $7.25 to $9.95
Dinner: $13.95 to $18.95

The Grill Room
(in the Ritz Carlton)
280 Vanderbilt Beach Road
Naples
(941) 598-6644
Hours: 6 P.M. to 10 P.M.
Features: seafood, steak; formal dining; entertainment
Dinner: $31 to $38

Michelbob's
371 Airport Road
Naples
(941) 643-2877
Hours: 11 A.M. to 9 P.M.
Features: great barbecue ribs and chicken, children's menu; casual dress; Sunday brunch
Lunch: $5 to $13
Dinner: $8 to $16

The Riverwalk Fish & Ale House
1200 5th Avenue South
Naples

(941) 263-2734

Hours: 11 A.M. to 11 P.M.

Features: seafood, sandwiches, children's menu; casual waterfront dining; outdoor seating available

Lunch: $7.95 to $19.95

Dinner: $7.95 to $19.95

Seawitch Fishmarket & Restaurant

179 Southbay Drive

Vanderbilt Beach

(941) 566-1514

Hours: 11:30 P.M. to 2:30 P.M., 5 P.M. to 9:30 P.M., light fare from 2:30 P.M. to 5 P.M.

Features: seafood, steak; casual waterfront dining

Lunch: $6 to $10

Dinner: $13 to $17

St. George & the Dragon

936 Fifth Avenue

Naples

(941) 262-6546

Hours: 11 A.M. to 10 P.M.; Sunday (January to March) until 9 P.M.

Features: seafood, steak, daily lunch and dinner specials; dinner jackets in main dining room, no shorts

Lunch: $4.95 to $12.95

Dinner: $10.50 to $38.95

Marco Island

Accommodations

☘ Marco Island Hilton Beach Resort

560 South Collier Boulevard
Marco Island, FL 34145
(941) 394-5000
(941) 394-5251 (fax)
(800) HILTONS

Every junior and one-bedroom suite at the Marco Island Hilton opens to a furnished terrace overlooking the lush, tropical pool setting and the ever-changing waters of the Gulf. The resort features several restaurants and a lounge with nightly entertainment. This world-class resort hotel is an exclusive retreat for discriminating travelers.

- TAC $$$
- 294 Units
- Suites
- Pool
- Hot Tub
- Color Cable TV
- Handicapped Access
- Restaurant/Bar
- Fitness Center
- Conference Facilities
- Fax Services
- Mastercard, VISA, Discover, American Express
- Check-in: 3 P.M. Check-out: 12 P.M.

☘ Marco Island Marriot Resort

400 South Collier Boulevard
Marco Island, FL 34145
(941) 394-2511
(941) 642-2672 (fax)
(800) GET-HERE

Marco Island Hilton Beach Resort

Marco Island Marriot Resort and Golf Club

The Marco Island Marriot is a huge resort with two high-rise towers, a variety of restaurants and bars, three pools, golf, lighted tennis courts, miniature golf, basketball, game room, and children's program.

- TAC $$$
- 735 Units
- Suites
- Pool
- Hot Tub
- Color Cable TV
- Guest Laundry
- Handicapped Access
- Restaurant/Bar
- Fitness Center
- Conference Facilities
- Fax Services
- Mastercard, VISA, Discover, American Express
- Check-in: 3 P.M. Check-out: 12 P.M.

Radisson Suite Beach Resort on Marco Island
600 South Collier Boulevard
Marco Island, FL 34145
(941) 394-4100
(941) 394-0419 (fax)
(800) 992-0651
http://www.ssrc.com

A sun-drenched aquatic playground awaits you at the Radisson Suite Beach Resort. This tropical paradise features all beachview accommodations and offers the finest recreation programs. The nicely furnished one- and two-bedroom suites have fully equipped kitchens and separate living rooms.

- TAC $$$
- 269 Units
- Hotel rooms; one- and two-bedroom suites with fully equipped kitchens
- Pool
- Hot Tub
- Color Cable TV
- Guest Laundry
- Handicapped Access
- Restaurant/Bar
- Shuffleboard
- Fitness Center
- Conference Facilities
- Fax Services
- Mastercard, VISA, Discover, American Express
- Check-in: 4 P.M. Check-out: 12 P.M.

Radisson Suite Beach Resort on Marco Island

Resort Rental Companies

Bluebill Vacation Properties, Inc.
Marco Island
(941) 992-6620
(941) 992-9552 (fax)
(800) 237-2010

Marco Beach Rentals, Inc.
Marco Island
(941) 642-5400
(941) 394-8639 (fax)
(800) 423-7809

Collier Seminole State Park & Boat Tours

20200 East Tamiami

Naples (8 miles from Marco Island)

(941) 642-8898

Canoe rentals, campgrounds, picnic areas, fishing, and 10,000 Island boat tours are available at this park. See wildlife in it natural habitat aboard a pontoon boat equipped with restrooms.

Hours: 9 A.M. to 5 P.M. (boat tour); park open from sunrise to sunset

Admission: Adults, $8.50; children ages 6 to 12, $5; children 5 and under, free

Marco Island Trolley Tours

First pick-up at the Marriot Hotel

(941) 394-1600

Narrated tour and shopping excursion around Marco Island. Includes historical tour of Caxambas and a stop at the Indian Mounds

Hours: Call for route, schedule, and prices

Dining Out

Apollo's Oceanview

900 South Collier Boulevard

Marco Island

(941) 389-0509

Hours: 11 A.M. to 2 P.M.; 5 P.M. to 9 P.M.; Sunday brunch, 11 A.M. to 2 P.M.; closed Monday

Features: continental cuisine, Sunday brunch, children's menu, outside beach bar (open 4 P.M.); casual waterfront dining

Lunch: $4.95 to $10 (lunch buffet includes salad and dessert bar for $8.50)

Dinner: $14.95 to $28.95

Snook Inn
1215 Bald Eagle Drive
Marco Island
(941) 394-3313
Hours: 11 A.M. to 10 P.M.
Features: fresh seafood, famous grouper sandwich; outdoor bar; casual riverfront dining; come by car or boat
Lunch: $6.75 to $8.50
Dinner: $7.75 to $18.95
Note: Wear Skin-So-Soft as "no-see-ums" are sometimes bothersome.

Voyager
400 South Collier Boulevard (Marriot's Marco Island Resort & Golf Club)
Marco Island
(941) 394-2511
Hours: 5:30 P.M. to 10 P.M.
Features: seafood, salad bar, children's menu, early bird specials; smartly casual dress
Dinner: $10.95 to $29.95

SOUTHWEST AREA GOLF
(Semi-private and Public)

Audubon Country Club
15725 North Tamiami Trail
Naples
(941) 597-2229
Semi-private; driving range, restaurant

Bay Beach Golf Club
7401 Estero Boulevard
Fort Myers Beach
(941) 463-2064
Public

Beachview Golf Club
1100 Parview Drive
Sanibel
(941) 472-2626
Semi-private; restaurant

Bonita Fairways
9751 West Terry Street
Bonita Springs
(941) 947-9100
Semi-private; driving range, restaurant

Bonita Springs Golf & Country Club
10200 Maddox Lane
Bonita Springs
(941) 992-2800
Semi-private; restaurant

Boyne South Country Club
18100 Royal Tree Parkway
Naples
(941) 774-5931
Public

Countryside Golf & Country Club
500 Countryside Drive
Naples
(941) 455-0001
Semi-private; driving range, restaurant

Cross Creek Country Club
13050 Cross Creek Boulevard
Fort Myers
(941) 768-1922
Semi-private; restaurant

Del Tura Country Club
18621 NorthTamiami Trail NW
North Fort Myers
(941) 731-4125
Semi-private; driving range, restaurant

Del Vera
18621 Tamiami Trail
North Fort Myers
(941) 731-4520
Semi-private; driving range, restaurant

Dunes Golf & Tennis Club
949 San Castle Road
Sanibel
(941) 472-3355
Semi-private; driving range, restaurant

Eastwood Golf Club
4600 Bruce Herd Lane
Fort Myers
(941) 275-488
Public; driving range, restaurant

El Rio Golf Club
1801 Skyline Drive
North Fort Myers
(941) 995-2204
Public; driving range, restaurant

Embassy Woods at Bretonne Park
6818 Davis Boulevard
Naples
(941) 353-1115
Semi-private

Fort Myers Country Club
3591 McGregor Boulevard
Fort Myers
(941) 936-2457
Public; restaurant

Gateway Golf Club
11360 Championship Drive
Fort Myers
(941) 561-1010
Semi-private; driving range, restaurant

Golden Gate Country Club
4100 Golden Gate Parkway
Naples
(941) 455-9498
Semi-private; driving range, restaurant

Golf Club at Marco
343 Marriott Club Drive
Naples
(941) 793-6060
Semi-private; driving range, restaurant

Gulf Harbour Yacht & Country Club
14700 Portsmouth Boulevard SW
Fort Myers
(941) 433-4211
Public; driving range

Hibiscus Golf Club
175 Doral Circle
Naples
(941) 774-0088
Semi-private; driving range, restaurant

Hunter's Ridge Golf Club
12500 Hunter's Ridge Drive
Bonita Springs
(941) 992-7667
Semi-private; driving range, restaurant

Ironwood Golf Club
205 Charity Court
Naples
(941) 775-2584
Public; restaurant

Kelly Greens
12300 Kelly Greens Boulevard SW
Fort Myers
(941) 466-9552
Semi-private; driving range, restaurant

Lely Resort - The Classics
8004 Lely Resort Boulevard
Naples
(941) 793-2600
Public

Lely Resort - Flamingo Island Club
12655 East Tamiami Trail
Naples
(941) 793-2600
Public

Lexington Country Club
1728 Winkler Road
Fort Myers
(941) 482-8828
Semi-private; driving range, restaurant

Lochmoor Country Club
3911 Orange Grove Boulevard
North Fort Myers
(941) 995-0501
Semi-private; driving range, restaurant

Marco Shores Golf Club
1450 Mainsail Drive
Marco Island
(941) 394-2581
Public; driving range, restaurant

Marriot's Marco Island Resort & Country Club
3433 Marriot Club Drive
Naples
(941) 793-6060
Public; driving range, restaurant

Naples Beach Hotel & Golf Club
851 Gulfshore Boulevard North
Naples
(941) 261-2222
Public; driving range, restaurant

Old Hickory Golf & Country Club
14670 Old Hickory Boulevard
Fort Myers
(941) 768-2400
Semi-private; driving range, restaurant

Palm River Country Club
Palm River Boulevard
Naples
(941) 597-3554
Semi-private; driving range, restaurant

Pine Lakes Country Club
19371 North Tamiami Trail
North Fort Myers
(941) 731-5565
Semi-private; driving range, restaurant

Riverbend Golf Club
6270 Walter Hagen Court NE
North Fort Myers
(941) 543-2200
Semi-private; driving range, restaurant

Riviera Golf Club
48 Marseilles Drive
Naples
(941) 774-1081
Public; restaurant

Sabal Springs Golf & Racquet Club LTD
3347 Sabal Springs Boulevard
North Fort Myers
(941) 731-2191
Semi-private; driving range, restaurant

South Seas Plantation
South Seas Plantation Road
Captiva
(941) 472-5111
Semi-private; driving range, restaurant

Worthington Country Club
13500 Worthington Way
Bonita Springs
(941) 495-1750
Semi-private; driving range, restaurant

CHAMBERS OF COMMERCE

Bonita Springs Chamber of Commerce
PO Box 747
Bonita Springs, FL 33959
(941) 992-2943
e-mail: bonita@coconet.com

Greater Fort Myers Beach Area Chamber of Commerce
17200 San Carlos Boulevard
Fort Myers Beach, FL 33931
(941) 454-7500
(800) 782-9283

Lee Island Coast Visitor and Convention Bureau
2180 West First Street, Suite 100
Fort Myers, FL 33901
(941) 338-3500
(800) 237-6444

Marco Island Area Chamber of Commerce
1102 North Collier Boulevard
Marco Island, FL 33937
(941) 394-7549
(800) 788-MARCO

Naples Area Chamber of Commerce
895 5th Avenue South
Naples, FL 33940
(941) 262-6141

Naples Area Tourism Bureau
PO Box 10129
Naples, FL 33941
(941) 262-2712
(800) 605-7878

Sanibel-Captiva Islands Chamber of Commerce
1159 Causeway Boulevard
Sanibel, FL 33957
(941) 472-1080

Lodgings That Accept Pets

Listed below are lodgings that accept pets. Please refer to the specific page numbers beside the accommodation names for details concerning any restrictions and/or fees the lodgings might have regarding pets. All pet deposits are refundable.

PANHANDLE BEACHES

Okaloosa Island/Fort Walton Beach
Ramada Plaza Beach Resort 14

Panama City Beach
Gulf Edge Inn 31
Parson's Place 36
Pineapple Beach Villas 36
Sandpiper-Beacon 38
Wind Drift Motel 41

Mexico Beach
Driftwood Inn 45
Sandman Motel 46

SUNCOAST BEACHES

Clearwater Beach
Clearwater Beach Hotel 59

Indian Rocks Beach
Sandy Shores Motel &
     Apartments 70

Indian Shores
Casa Chica Cottages 75
Edgewater Beach Resort 77
Fairwind Cottages 77
La Regina Motel 80

Madeira Beach
The Schooner Motel on the Gulf
     91

Treasure Island
Captain's Quarters Inn 98
Seahorse Cottages 102

SARASOTA/MANATEE BEACHES

Anna Maria Island (Including Holmes Beach and Bradenton Beach)
Aquarius Beach Resort 126
The Breakers 127
Sandy Toes 130

Index of Accommodations

If you enjoyed reading this book, here are some other books from Pineapple Press on related topics. For a complete catalog, write to Pineapple Press, P.O. Box 3899, Sarasota, FL 34230, or call 1-800-PINEAPL (746-3275).

Florida Island Hopping: The West Coast by Chelle Koster Walton. The first tour guide to Florida's Gulf coast barrier islands, including their histories, unique characters, and complete information on natural attractions, shopping, touring, and other diversions.

The Mostly Mullet Cookbook: A Culinary Celebration of the South's Favorite Fish by George "Grif" Griffin. Grif delights every palate with recipes that are simple, healthful, and — most importantly — do justice to this gastronomic gift from the sea.

The Surfer's Guide to Florida by Amy Vansant. In this first comprehensive guide to the surf breaks in the Sunshine State, you will find information on the locations, swell conditions, and particulars of nearly 200 of Florida's best waves.

Sea Kayaking in Florida by David Gluckman. Whether you want to fish or just watch wildlife, sea kayaking offers new ways to enjoy Florida's hidden bays and open oceans.

Seashore Plants of South Florida and the Caribbean by David W. Nellis. A complete source of information for backyard gardeners, beach wanderers, and serious naturalists about which plants grow best in nearshore environments.

Guide to Florida Lighthouses by Elinor De Wire. Thirty lighthouses guide ships along Florida's coasts. This elegant book, with full-color photos, traces the story of each.

Florida's Birds: A Handbook and Reference by Herbert W. Kale II, David S. Maehr, and Karl Karalus. This guide to the identification, enjoyment, and protection of Florida's beautiful population of birds identifies and discusses over 325 species, with information on distinguishing marks, habitat, season, and distribution.

The Nature of Things on Sanibel by George R. Campbell. Written by a man who truly knows and loves the Island, this book acquaints the reader with the plants, animals, people, and places that make Sanibel the remarkable place it is.